THE DISH

Also by Andrew Friedman

*Chefs, Drugs and Rock & Roll: How Food Lovers,
Free Spirits, Misfits and Wanderers Created a New
American Profession*

*Knives at Dawn: America's Quest for Culinary Glory
at the Legendary Bocuse d'Or Competition*

*Don't Try This at Home: Culinary
Catastrophes from the World's Greatest Chefs*
(co-editor, with Kimberly Witherspoon)

THE DISH

The Lives and Labor
Behind One Plate of Food

ANDREW FRIEDMAN

MARINER BOOKS
New York   Boston

THE DISH. Copyright © 2023 by Andrew Friedman. All rights
reserved. Printed in the United States of America. No part of
this book may be used or reproduced in any manner whatsoever
without written permission except in the case of brief quotations
embodied in critical articles and reviews. For information, address
HarperCollins Publishers, 195 Broadway, New York, NY 10007.

HarperCollins books may be purchased for educational, business,
or sales promotional use. For information, please email the
Special Markets Department at SPsales@harpercollins.com.

FIRST EDITION

Designed by Renata DiBiase

Library of Congress Cataloging-in-Publication Data has been applied for.

ISBN 978-0-06-313597-0

23 24 25 26 27 LBC 5 4 3 2 1

In memory of three friends lost during
the year I worked on this book:

Marcia Nasatir, Tom Perrotta, and Eddie Schoenfeld,
who shared, respectively, my love of movies, tennis,
and restaurants, and whose passion, intelligence,
and humanity continue to guide and inspire me.

And for the food professionals who've
trusted me to tell their stories.

The difference between a cow and a bean is a bean
can begin an adventure.

—STEPHEN SONDHEIM

The same people who cook it
when I'm in the kitchen!

—attributed to chef PAUL BOCUSE, in response to a
restaurant guest asking who cooked their food when Bocuse
visited the dining room

Show a little faith, there's magic in the night.

—BRUCE SPRINGSTEEN

Contents

Author's Note

This all really happened.
I just moved a few things around.

Introduction:
How Does It All Fit Together?

The great, albeit fictional, parapsychologist Fox Mulder once theorized that dreams answer questions that we don't know how to ask.

The idea for this book came to me in a dream. I woke up one morning with the concept fully formed: to select one dish, in one restaurant, and profile the people—in the restaurant and beyond its walls—whose lives and work culminate on the plate. The question posed by the dream was: *How does it all fit together?*

It was a query I couldn't answer, even unconsciously. That was the point. If I wanted to answer it, I'd have to research and write the book.

I've been reporting and broadcasting about chefs and kitchen culture for close to twenty-five years. During that time, I've observed hospitality professionals during both prep and service; interviewed or casually gabbed with everyone from the chefs to the dishwashers in well over a hundred places; visited farms, sometimes for an overnight stay; and been privileged to enjoy thousands of lunches and dinners, and often to discuss them with the people who conceived and prepared them. I have been privy to every building block of a meal, but couldn't tell you with specificity how to snap together the pieces that made up any single dish: By what means of communication and instruction are new recipes and dishes disseminated to cooks? How do farmers determine what to grow and how much, process orders from dozens of chef-customers, and organize and execute their packing and delivery obligations? Exactly when and how do kitchens purchase produce and proteins (fish and meats)? And by what synchronous miracle do multiple cooks achieve the feat of having the disparate components of a single dish ready at the same time and at the correct individual temperatures, while also executing myriad other tasks in the pressure cooker of a service?

If I couldn't answer these questions, what did the average restaurant patron know about what it took to produce their meals? Taking it a step further: Did any of us really understand precisely how much work, creativity, and collaboration were represented on even just one plate?

To find out, I followed the dream's dictate and worked backward from a single dish, forensically tracing its construction along two tracks: the individual contributions of members of the kitchen and dining room teams, and the work undertaken by farmers and purveyors to grow, raise, and process the key ingredients that comprise the dish.

After a search conducted from my home office during the COVID-19 pandemic, I settled on Chicago's Wherewithall restaurant as the focal point. Because Wherewithall exclusively serves a set (or tasting) menu that changes weekly, and the chefs create best under the gun, I didn't know what the dish would be until I was on the ground at the beginning of the penultimate week of July 2021, which I spent observing there. (This may sound like a high-wire decision, but I made my selection based on the restaurant's people and practices and so was comfortable with it.) To allow for maximum narrative runway, the plan was to make the final savory course, which at Wherewithall is always centered on poultry or meat, the titular focus of the book. As it turned out, that week's meat course, as christened on the menu, was *Dry-Aged Strip Loin, Tomato, Sorrel*.

Johnny Clark and Beverly Kim, the husband-and-wife chef team who own Wherewithall, granted me extraordinary access to its workspace, dining room, and staff, and helped me connect with the farmers, rancher, and vintner whose wares comprise the dish. In addition to my week at the restaurant observing and interviewing several employees, I spent a second, nonconsecutive week driving around the Midwest in a rental car, touring farms and production facilities, riding shotgun on a delivery run, and interviewing proprietors and field workers.

It was an adventure, and an education. I hope it proves to be the same for you.

Andrew Friedman
Brooklyn, NY
January 2023

1

Calling Orders

Holly Knox, host of Wherewithall, a fifty-seat restaurant of steel, glass, blond wood, and exposed brick, leans in its doorway, eyes trained skyward at clouds, dark as doom, gathering over Chicago, eclipsing the sun. The forecast failed to predict it, but at 4:30 P.M., this midsummer day has apocalyptically become night, and there's no question a storm is going to—

Fuck! The aerial dam has burst, and here it is already. Just like *that*, the city is under hydra-assault: Strangers huddle close under awnings. Cars decelerate to a wary crawl. Raindrops splatter like water balloons against Wherewithall's rectangular bank of dining-room windows, turning the view from within impressionistic. Inside, in anticipation of the night's first guests, a handful of servers costumed in crisp white dress shirts and blue aprons zhoosh the dining room. In the open

kitchen, a trio of cooks load for bear, stocking lowboys*
with trays of butchered fish and meat, their stations
with extra side towels. Everyone presses ahead in de-
nial of the deluge, until a leak in the kitchen ceiling
forces the issue. A team member races upstairs to the
gutted vacant apartment above and secures a linoleum
square over a breach in the floorboards, impeding the
flow—a stopgap in an age of stopgaps.

It's Saturday, July 24, 2021, and Wherewithall—
like most surviving restaurants—could use a break. The
COVID-19 pandemic has plagued (literally) society
for more than a year, forcing a nationwide industry
shutdown that began in March 2020, and to date has
claimed close to 100,000 American restaurants and
bars, along with more than four million lives worldwide. In recent months, vaccines have been making
their way into arms (especially in liberal strongholds
like Chicago) and, with worrying variants yet to materialize, life has been lurching toward normal, including
a guarded revival of indoor restaurant dining. Johnny
Clark and Beverly Kim, the married couple who are the
restaurant's co-chefs and own both the restaurant and
the building that houses it, recently stopped requiring
staff to wear microbe-impeding surgical-style masks.
Still, on pleasant evenings they keep the back door,

---

* small refrigerators positioned beneath kitchen work counters

Johnny Clark and Beverly Kim
Photograph by Cory Dewald. Used by permission of Parachute restaurant.

which leads to a cozy concrete courtyard and a private event space and office on its far side, open for the reassurance of ventilation, which now won't be possible for hours.

Wherewithall has reservations for ninety-two customers in the system tonight, the most since reopening four weeks earlier—an opportunity for the staff to continue reconditioning and for the restaurant to inhale life-sustaining revenue. But furious weather prompts cancellations even in sturdier times, so that's all suddenly tentative until five-fifty, ten minutes ahead of opening, when the last, lingering drizzle tapers off and the sun makes a steamy encore before true evening falls. Around the corner on residential North Albany Avenue, toddlers and stoop sitters reemerge from modest houses packed into overgrown subdivided lots, and somewhere down there a lone songbird chirps, marking itself safe. For now things have taken a beneficent turn, and Wherewithall and its team have all anyone could ask or expect of the summer of '21: a chance.

An hour later and the storm has receded like a bad dream. Or was the storm the reality, and is *this* the dream? It sure seems illusory: the long-dormant dining room reanimated with unselfconscious human interaction; the barroom, where Holly checks guests in on a touchscreen tablet fixed to a freestanding podium, flowering into a pageant of reunion and celebration:

> *"Let's have a drink here before we sit down."*
> *"Frank! How long has it been?"* *"Since the pandemic, at least."* *"Give us a hug . . . if it feels safe."*
> *"Happy birthday, you!"*

The two adjacent rooms, joined by a doorless passageway lined with slatted wood in imitation of a wine cask's interior, thrum with music. Each night, general manager Jessica Line (mid-thirties, frizzy auburn hair) selects a "radio station"* on Spotify based on the distinguishing characteristics of a different artist. Tonight, in homage to co-chef-owner Johnny's hometown, it's Heartless Bastards, a Cincinnati, Ohio, rock band whose honky-tonk sound is deconstructed and extrapolated to a hodgepodge of rock, bluegrass, country, and soul. Right now, Nashville's Lilly Hiatt trills of love and devotion in "Brightest Star."

Beverly and Johnny own and operate two restaurants. They launched their first, Parachute—whose building they also own—a block and a half away in May 2014; the à la carte menu there refracts American-born Beverly's Korean heritage through the prism of her and Johnny's classical Western (read: French) culinary training. Five years later, they opened Wherewithall, where the cuisine is more expansively modern American, which is to say that it draws on a panoply of cultures and cuisines, sometimes riffing on traditional preparations or dishes. The couple are also prolific in other ways, with three young children ages three, four, and eleven, and a dog—a Bordeaux mastiff named François who wears a permanent jowly expression of

---

* an arch way of referring to a playlist generated by an algorithm or third party

ennui. Occasionally, in the hours before dinner service, the six of them come romping into the restaurant like a modern *Family Circus* reboot, and the kids color at the bar or chase each other around the courtyard while their parents grapple with the vast, never-ending miscellany of chefdom and proprietorship.

Both Parachute and Wherewithall occupy the category of restaurants shorthanded as *chef-driven*, *destination*, or even—despite their relative casualness—*fine-dining*. They are independent, but not mom-and-pop. Instead of standards available in thousands of other restaurants, most of the dishes here are unique, conceived as much for the expression of the chefs—including the restaurant's chef de cuisine,* Tayler Ploshehanski—as for the nourishment, satisfaction, and entertainment of the guests. Years before they met, Beverly and Johnny both tournéed their way through prestigious cooking schools, then sharpened their skills and palates in heralded kitchens—she at, among others, the landmark American dining temple Charlie Trotter's in Chicago; he at the historic La Côte Basque and others in New York City. They retain a publicist who hawks them to the media, and are represented by an agent who ferrets out television opportunities.

---

* Chef de cuisine is the day-to-day chef of a restaurant. When used, the title usually describes a chef who manages the kitchen and creates the menu in consultation or collaboration with the chef-owner(s) whose vision dictates the restaurant's culinary style.

They are frequently written about; Parachute holds a Michelin star; and Beverly and Johnny jointly received a James Beard Foundation Award (foodlandia's Oscar) as Best Chef of the Great Lakes region. Beverly also has been a *cheftestant* on the long-running Bravo TV cooking competition series *Top Chef*. In their industry, they are one-percenters.

And yet Wherewithall is, in its way, egalitarian, down to the dress code, which doesn't exist. Were you to report for dinner in shorts and flip-flops, not an eye would bat, unless perhaps it was winter. Moreover, the restaurant serves a comparatively inexpensive set (or tasting) menu—meaning that guests of wildly varying backgrounds and means consume the same sequence of seven courses, five savory and two sweet, with an optional cheese selection bridging those realms. Each week's menu features two snacks (the quotidian English word currently overtaking the French *amuses* as the preferred designation for one- or two-bite welcome treats from the kitchen); broth, bread, and butter; a grains course; a fish course; a meat course; an intermezzo (pre-dessert); and dessert. Except for the bread and butter, the lineup changes weekly, with tweaks made day to day as ingredient availability and the chefs' contentment with the dishes dictate, and with modifications at the ready to accommodate allergies and the animal averse.

WHEREWITHALL DINNER MENU
July 24, 2021

snacks
(*not featured on printed menu*)

broth, bread, and butter
(*not featured on printed menu*)

oats, button chanterelles, baby corn
mari vineyards 2016 riesling, mi

hake, wax beans, vin jaune
holger koch, 2020 grauburgunder + others, de

dry-aged strip loin, tomato, sorrel
wyncroft 2017 cabernet sauvignon + others, mi

intermezzo
(*not featured on printed menu*)

roasted peaches, lemon custard, chamomile
rare wine co. madeira, pt

nightly menu	$85
wine pairing	$45
today's cheese	$15
(johan 2014 visdom chardonnay)	$15

The food, like the food at most restaurants, is the creative, technical, and physical work product of not just Johnny, Beverly, and chef de cuisine Tayler, but also of their sous chef and cooks, dishwashing team, and servers. From beyond the restaurant, it contains the labor of farmers, farmhands, producers, delivery people, packers, and too many others to list in full. That's as true for any one dish as it is for the meal.

Take, for example, the meat course—*our* dish—on which we'll focus for the next seventy-five minutes of Wherewithall time, tracking its preparation amid the kitchen tumult, like the unnamed girl in the red dress, unmissable against the otherwise black-and-white canvas of *Schindler's List*. Along the way, we'll meet the people who contribute to it, both inside the restaurant and at the farms that provide its defining ingredients.

As they will the other six components of the meal, the kitchen will cook, plate, and serve the meat course ninety-two times tonight. After a current fashion, it's minimally and modestly (note the lowercase letters) summarized on the menu: *dry-aged strip loin, tomato, sorrel*. That's all most guests likely to dine at a restaurant like Wherewithall in 2021 need to know. They will rightly assume that *dry-aged strip loin, tomato, sorrel* will arrive on a dinner plate bearing some treatment of the three promised ingredients and augmented by supporting elements. In this case, a portion of the strip loin will be roasted, sliced, and laid atop a spattering of red wine reduction—a winery-produced blend of Cabernet Sauvignon, Cabernet Franc, and Merlot from Michigan's Wyncroft that's been given a makeover in the Wherewithall kitchen, emerging enriched with butterfat and redolent of onions and herbs. If there's a curveball, it's the scale of the tomato: half a purplish-red baseball of a Brandywine that's been split across its equator, exposing the fruit within, and patiently dehydrated in an oven for hours—not to the point of desiccation, but just enough to concentrate its juices and intensify its tomato-ness. It will be sauced with a ladleful of that red wine reduction, require a knife and fork, and occupy an allotment of real estate commensurate to that of the beef. The sorrel, in starkest contrast, will appear in the form of three or four unadorned leaves per serving, draped over and against the tomato, like those molten clocks in Dali's *Persistence of Memory*. (In these moments before service commences, the building blocks of our dish are stashed around the kitchen and mostly out of sight: Butchered segments of strip loin of varying sizes are wrapped in plastic, with the number of four-ounce portions each will yield scribbled on the plastic in blue Sharpie.

Our dish: Wherewithall's meat course—Dry-Aged Strip
Loin, Tomato, Sorrel—served July 20–24, 2021

Picked sorrel leaves are gathered in a cube-shaped
Lexan* kept, with the lid tightly fastened, in a lowboy
refrigerator to prevent their wilting in the kitchen's
ambient heat. The components of the red wine sauce
are also kept there. Halved, semi-dehydrated tomatoes
are gathered on cooling racks over sheet trays in the
open kitchen.)

* A Lexan is an extremely durable food container made of polycarbonate resin
thermoplastic. Lexans are manufactured in various sizes and are prevalent in
professional kitchens.

Yes, dozens of workers across untold months and miles collaborated to bring even such an elemental composition to the plate.

Here, see for yourself . . .

As darkness and moonlight flood the sky outside, the neon of Chief O'Neill's Irish pub across the street, promising Guinness and free Wi-Fi, catches and shimmies in the puddles on this industrial stretch of North Elston Avenue, a main thoroughfare of the city's working-class Avondale area. (Under a nearby underpass, a weathered Works Progress Administration–style black and white mural depicts a bricklayer, above whom it proclaims *Avondale: The Neighborhood That Built Chicago*.) Inside Wherewithall, general manager Jessica dims the lights and turns up the volume, and the crowd morphs younger, dressed for a Big Night, their plumage supplanting the early birds' madras and pastels, the likelihood of postprandial coupling palpably elevated. By eight o'clock—the epicenter of Saturday night service—the dining room, for the first time in more than a year, nears capacity, with still more guests waiting in the barroom; the instant a party* signs their

---

* In restaurant parlance, the occupants of a table collectively constitute a party; each meal served is a cover.

The little neighborhood that could

credit card slip and decamps, their table is cleared, sanitized (a COVID-era adaptation), reset, and repopulated.

In the open kitchen, visible and audible to the dining room, the cooks are in octopus mode; passing by, you'd do well to isolate a detail or two: A brawny, bearded man and a trim, curly locked, slightly younger cook dancing around each other in the narrow strip of space between the ovens and the pass, the counter on which finished dishes are arrayed for servers to gather them before shuttling them to their respective tables. (Servers announce themselves on arrival here with whispers of "hands," meaning theirs are unencumbered, free to ferry plates or bowls. It recalls peewee football receivers hailing a quarterback: *"I'm open! I'm open!"*) The curly headed cook has four small saucepans working on the stovetop and something going on in the ovens beneath; the bearded one slices white-fleshed fish fillets into portions, sneaking frequent glances at the digital thermometer that monitors the doneness of whatever's in the refrigerator-sized oven behind him. There are just three dedicated cooks working service, and these two prepare most of the dishes. Another man, the restaurant's polisher, a white painter's cap skewed loosely on his head, replenishes piles of dishes and clusters of glasses on the shelves and in the cubbyholes built into and around the kitchen and bar. From a separate workstation off to the side comes the third cook, a woman in her early twenties who sets two earthenware bowls on the pass, takes a single giant stride back to her area, then pivots and returns in a flash with a wire basket filled snugly with sliced bread and a small plate bearing house-made butter. The cooks constitute a three-person three-ring circus, the performers endlessly repeating their intermittently intersecting routines.

There's no door to the kitchen, just a gap where the pass ends, and there stands Tayler, the chef de cuisine. Tayler is thirty-two. Her dirty-blond hair has been piled atop her head and wrangled into a scrunchy. Gargantuan glasses frame her face, suggesting an egghead, which is funny because the adjective she most often applies to herself is *silly,* which also is funny because her kitchen self—white jacket, roving eyes, mechanical pencil perennially poised at the ready—radiates seriousness. A gauzy white bandage, snug as papier-mâché, hugs her left hand where she sliced herself earlier in the day, just hours from escaping the week unscathed. (The restaurant is closed on Sundays and Mondays.)

Like a boulder around and over which a white river rages, Tayler may be the only staff member not racing about. In the dining room, hosts shepherd guests to tables; servers dispense advice, enthusiasm, food, and drink; diners dine. In the bar, cocktails are concocted; wine is poured; bottles are retrieved from cube-shaped refrigerators, glowing from recesses in the wall overhead. In the kitchen, the crew generate the same handful of courses over and over, like a musical round.

The heartbeat of Wherewithall's kitchen is the handoff of a chit—a three by five-inch rectangle of thermal paper—from server to chef. This transaction prompts the staggered preparation of all the dishes for a party, whether one guest or six. When the restaurant does robust business, the heart pumps constantly and orders flow incessantly, metronomically (*fingers-crossed emoji!*),

Chef de cuisine Tayler Ploshehanski expedites at the end of a busy week.

one behind the other, nudging each other along; on a busy night, at any given moment, a few dozen dishes will be in various states of preparation. This makes tracking the progress of a single dish from start to finish—as we are about to do with *Dry-Aged Strip Loin, Tomato, Sorrel*—a mindboggling proposition, unless we home in on a newly arrived chit and the Rube Goldbergian chain reaction it initiates.

And so, there's Nooshâ Elami, one of Wherewithall's four servers on duty tonight: an extroverted Iranian American in her early thirties, dark black hair gathered in a ponytail, features accentuated by mascara, gold hoop earrings, and overlapping gold and silver necklaces

Nooshâ Elami confers with chef-owner Johnny Clark at the pass.

dangling. It's now about a quarter past eight and she's at Table 12, a deuce[*] along one of two columns of tables separated by an enormous rectangular planter lush with jade pothos plants, banquette seating built onto three of its sides. Waiting for her there are a man and a woman—clearly a couple—in their early forties, chattering away. Nooshâ delivers a cocktail, The Last Word (made here with mezcal), for him, and a glass of Riesling for her.

"I don't see any allergies or aversions on your reservation," says Nooshâ, scanning their chit. "Is that right?" (At Wherewithall, chits are preprinted and

[*] table for two

paperclipped to each party's menus at the host podium where they're kept in a small box. They are given to the server when the corresponding party arrives and is seated. If applicable, allergies and aversions would have been captured in the online reservation notes or over the phone, and reflected on its chit. But there's no harm in redundancy here since the consequences of a true allergy include . . . well . . . *death*.)

"Anything goes," says the man, grinning ingratiatingly. "Let it rip."

Had modifications been necessary, Nooshâ would have annotated the chit by hand, indicating which member(s) of the party they applied to, according to position number (place at the table). For example, "P1 celiac" or "P2 veg" (for vegetarian); this system enables the kitchen to be sure servers deliver bespoke dishes to their rightful diner.

Offstage, Nooshâ presents as confident and authoritative. In the dining room, she prides herself on calibrating her service style to suit each party in her care: With obvious "foodies," she toplines food descriptions, lest she imply that a proud foodie doesn't know their rouille from their romesco. To enthusiastic novices—her favorite—she spoon-feeds primers on esoteric ingredients and preparations, offers wine pairing recommendation(s), and invites questions. Over the years, she's developed an intuition for who's who: "I don't think about it," she says. "It's hard to even describe how I know, but that's something that makes a good server—you know what a table needs. It's their body language, how they're looking at me, how interested they seem, what else is going on at the table." Nooshâ herself is a gastronome, game to try anything, with the idiosyncratic exception of lunch meats, to which she confesses a life-long aversion. A natural predisposition toward hunger makes her especially voracious. She also appreciates a glass of quality wine or a well-balanced cocktail. These predilections contribute to her ability to key into and connect with guests' culinary literacy or lack thereof.

The child of a midwestern American mother and Iranian father, Nooshâ was well acquainted with in-gredients and dishes that were alien to childhood contemporaries in her hometown of Grosse Point, Michigan. Both sides of her family had an affinity for Persian food, prompting cameos by pomegranate seeds and tahdig (buttery pan-fried rice) at their otherwise traditional American Thanksgiving and Christmas feasts. She herself also cooked: Her grandmother gifted her recipe books and a subscription to *Taste of Home*, which Nooshâ recalls as "the most Midwest cooking magazine you could ever get." At twelve, she made her first foray to the stove, emerging an hour later with chicken cacciatore. It took; thereafter, she seized every opportunity to prepare food for friends, at her home or theirs. As an adult living on her own, she throws frequent dinner parties and produces Thanksgiving and Christmas gatherings.

These joyous moments stand out in an otherwise pained adolescence: As a young child, Nooshâ moved with her family to Mattawan, Michigan, a small village southwest of Kalamazoo. There she experienced her first brush with racism, which intensified incalculably after Al-Qaeda's September 11, 2001, terrorist attacks on New York City and the Pentagon. Being of Iranian descent, with brown skin and an otherly name, she bore the local brunt of tribal antipathy toward anyone of Middle Eastern heritage that infected the United States that fall. Her eighth-grade classmates launched an Anti-Nooshâ Club; their secret hand gestures and explicit AIM messages conveyed the same grisly wish: *Nooshâ Elami should kill herself.* Not one classmate broke ranks to befriend—or even defend—her, and her appeals to the school administration drew limp platitudes. "I am being truly bullied by hundreds of kids every single day," Nooshâ pleaded. "Kids will be kids," shrugged the authorities.

For years, she passed weekday afternoons in self-imposed house arrest—a cruel sentence for a girl who, in her own words, was *addicted* to attention and had once been a class clown, in part to offset a tumultuous home life. (She unhesitatingly describes her mother and father as "bad parents," though doesn't volunteer details.) And here she was deprived of any positive regard. She claims a thick skin and innate self-confidence and resilience, capable of brushing off any rejection as "their loss." But what defenses wouldn't be worn thin by such unmerited and absolute antipathy?

"I don't want to say it didn't affect me," she says. "Obviously, it did. I was very depressed, and it was really difficult."

This might explain a dichotomy Nooshâ displays. She can come off as hard-shelled and coiled, someone on whose bad side you wouldn't want to find yourself. But she's also a softie. During the restaurant's COVID-driven temporary closure, she kept in touch with fellow women of Wherewithall via group text, expressing how much she missed work with messages like, "I honestly would love to be at preshift* right now."

After high school came Hope College, a small, private Christian liberal arts school, to which she was awarded a creative writing scholarship on the strength of her poetry and short stories. She felt no affinity for Hope, matriculating there only because her parents were alumni—an educational arranged marriage. She dropped out after a year and a half, then tried community college.

---

* a restaurant's nightly pre-service meeting

She didn't finish. But during those same years, she *did* flourish off the academic grid working in food-service. As a teen, she had staffed the counter at a Marble Slab Creamery (a predecessor to the similar Cold Stone Creamery) franchise and in 2012, during a brief post-college term of residency in Boston, took her first bona fide restaurant job, as host at a steakhouse, before returning to the Midwest and settling in Chicago.

Seven years and countless gigs later, Nooshâ started at Wherewithall in late summer 2019, right after the restaurant's debut that July. She came to the job following a string of others that began after Moto, a prominent modernist cuisine outpost where she'd waited tables, closed in 2016, following the suicide by hanging of its chef, Homaro Cantu. Nooshâ had flourished there, delivering cutting-edge food to the culinarily curious, many of whom treated their visits with the reverence of churchgoers.

"It was kind of similar to here where all the guests who came in knew what they were coming in for, so they were really excited," she says. "It was really easy to get along with them, and I loved talking to them about the food and the wine."

She found Wherewithall "calming," and the bright, airy space was a salve after her most recent short-lived assignment—a hipster bar in an unfailingly dark lair where it always felt like two A.M. She also appreciated

Beverly and Johnny's progressive proprietorship: The couple voluntarily provide what they can to their employees, including offering health insurance—by no means a given in the hospitality trade. They also lend their names, restaurants, and time to a variety of causes such as The Abundance Setting, a not-for-profit organization they co-founded to support working mothers in the industry. During the week I spent at the restaurant, a Brazilian woman who managed social media for the organization as a volunteer was trailing in the kitchen during the prep day. Beverly had invited her to spend time there to help the woman overcome a fear of working in fine dining. In support of another organization's mission, Beverly personally delivered meals for the not-for-profit Inspiration Kitchens, and she and Jessica spent part of their first meeting of the week making sure CSA (community-supported agriculture) deliveries to six mothers in need had been arranged. The restaurant itself occasionally wears its chef-owners' progressive worldview on its sleeve; for example, rather than specify gender, signs posted outside the bathroom doors indicate TWO TOILETS on one, and ONE URINAL AND ONE TOILET on the other.

Nooshâ attributes the dismissals and resignations implicit in her employment history to industry dynamics: "In almost all service industry jobs, everyone is getting treated like shit," she says, her voice quickening and laced with furious sarcasm. "You're getting treated like shit by your employers and by the people who come in, and [the mindset is that] you're supposed to take this abuse and, *actually*, you should be thankful for it. And when a guest is, like, 'Fuck you. I hate you. Here's zero dollars [for a tip],' you should smile at them and say, 'Thank you so much! Have a great day!'"

She says Wherewithall is the only job where she hasn't in some way been sexually or physically harassed, assaulted, and/or abused, including by customers whose innuendos and advances—like their insults—management expected her to absorb. But when she's working in a restaurant she loves (and she *loves* Wherewithall) she's in her element.

"I think attention to detail is really important," she says, "the ability to multitask and stay organized, and being able to know exactly all of your next steps and think about it without it stressing you out." All of that comes naturally to her. She aspires to greater patience and wishes she didn't find difficult guests emotionally draining, though does take satisfaction in cheering the occasional unhappy party.

Nooshâ plans to remain in her chosen trade. She desires advancement, but not ownership. She once considered it, but has come to value and prioritize downtime, personal pursuits, and sleep—impossible on what she believes, correctly, is the required 24/7 commitment of

restaurant proprietorship. In fact, quite the opposite—
she cherishes the ability to shut off the work spigot
when she clocks out: "I come into work. I'm at work. I
leave work. I never think about it. I love it."

Nooshâ walks the chit for Table 12 to the kitchen,
and hands it to Tayler, who visually scans it for any
annotations. Tayler spends most of her night in the
role of expediter, in which she directs, conducts, and
manages the cooks and their output, and functions as
a conduit between kitchen and dining room teams. Responsibilities for food quality and air traffic rest with
the expediter, who calls orders to the *brigade*,* listens
for the response (confirmation), and then tracks and
conducts, in the orchestral sense, the progress of each
dish, including checking each plate or bowl before
it leaves the pass and dispatching servers to deliver
dishes to their rightful tables. After initially calling the
order, the expediter will regularly communicate with
the dining room team to gauge where each table is in the
consumption of each course and instruct the cooks to
fire (finish) the next one so it's ready when guests antic-
ipate it. The role demands continual filtering of visual
and verbal data through the expediter's experience and

* the traditional French word for a kitchen team

intuition, and summed up for the cooks in a simple, direct command:

"Fire two *amuses*," calls Tayler, using the traditional name for snacks.

"Two *amuses*," confirms Jenna Cole, the young woman we noticed earlier shuttling crudité, bread, and butter. Jenna is twenty-three, the youngest crew member, tall of build and round of face, and moves with long strides and precise gestures. She's stationed at the back end of a side counter, where there's a little hand sink and the room bends round to a second kitchen that's concealed from guests' view. Jenna works *garmo*, nonexclusive house vernacular for "garde manger," traditionally defined as the station responsible for salads and cold appetizers. At Wherewithall, *garmo* produces the two-bite snacks that open each meal; readies the broth, bread, and house-churned butter that feature in each week's menu; and assembles cheese plates. Accordingly, her station setup includes a scale, a cutting board, and a sleek silver tea kettle that rests on a freestanding induction burner that's as slim and silvery as a MacBook Air.

This call-and-response is the preferred means of kitchen communication in tasting menu restaurants like Wherewithall. All parties have signed on for the same progression of dishes, so the expediter need only refer to courses by category, with the aforementioned possible accommodations—tonight, the beef broth may be replaced with a caramelized onion broth fashioned from a vegetable base; the fish course can be prepared with a wedge of roasted Caraflex cabbage in place of hake, the meat course with a plump porcini mushroom that the cooks will faintly score with the tip of a paring knife, roast, and baste with butter to make up for the fat that vanished with the beef. There's also that optional cheese course, which for $15 will be served between the meat and intermezzo (pre-dessert); for another $15, a glass of Johan Vineyards 2014 Visdom Chardonnay will be poured alongside said cheese.

Every restaurant has a system of tracking the progression of each party's courses and the status of their preparation. Here, progress is monitored on an expediting sheet, the kitchen's living sheet music, composed on a rolling basis nightly. It's a simple grid, with different-colored bands running across the 8 1/2 by 11-inch pages, oriented and printed horizontally (i.e., landscape). The structure of the menu at Wherewithall is always the same, so while dishes change week to week, the expediting categories don't. Across the top are column headers that name the courses, plus one on the left for table numbers and one on the right for notes. As the expediter calls each course for a table, they slash a diagonal line through that course's box on the grid. When the dish has departed the pass, the expediter draws a

Wherewithall's expediting sheets may be decidedly
low-tech, but they never glitch or crash.

diagonal line that bisects the first one, creating an *X* and
ushering that dish into the past. When the last *X* has
been completed in the last table's final dessert course,
the night's service is done.

The sheet and its maintenance facilitate order and so,
like the nuclear football, it's never unattended. There's
no official designation, but a handful of kitchen and
dining room team members are deputized to expedite
when Tayler needs to leave the pass to pitch in on the
line or, since the restaurant is currently without a pastry
chef, to plate desserts. Naturally Beverly and Johnny
can expedite, as can general manager Jessica; José Vil-

lalobos (late twenties; Mexican born, Chicago raised), Parachute's general manager, pitching in here—mostly as a server—while his usual domain undergoes renovations undertaken to make lemonade out of COVID; and a server or two. All are qualified air traffic controllers. (There's no vocal hand-off of the conn from one ranking officer to another; senior staff instinctively step in, like water coursing into a void, when they notice Tayler stepping away.) There's no rack or place on the pass for chits, as there are in some kitchens; instead they are gathered in a small, rectangular stainless-steel container for reference in case of confusion. (Other items kept within reach on the pass: a plastic cup packed with extra writing implements, and a box of birthday candles and a lighter, for celebratory desserts.) Similarly, notations are made in pencil on the expediting sheet to facilitate any corrections. When it gets busy there will be two or more sheets; right now, there are *four*, in two-by-two formation. The expediters draw thick horizontal lines with markers to group tables whose courses are running on a proximate schedule, enabling the kitchen to consolidate their efforts, and for multiple servers to deliver courses to more than one table simultaneously. And so it appears that each table in the dining room operates on its own schedule, when even on nights boasting close to one hundred covers, the kitchen is "only" readying a few groupings at any time.

The last course on the sheet is termed "MADS." It's shorthand for madeleines—spongy little cake-like ovals, usually served warm and often flavored gently with lemon. But the restaurant doesn't serve madeleines, at least not every week. The word became house style for mignardises or petits fours—the bite-sized sweets that put a button on the meal and help the check go down smoothly—when it was typed on an early iteration of the sheet, and never changed.* On this night, the final bites are Andes mint–sized rectangles of nougat.

When the time comes to fire each course that follows the *amuse*, Tayler will call it to Reuben Tomlins, the trim, curly-haired line cook, and Thomas Hollensed, the bearded one, who's the sous chef (second in command). But the pair don't wait for that moment to start them: When Tayler calls the first two snacks for any party, the entire team takes note. So though she's technically speaking only to Jenna, each time Tayler calls for the firing of an *amuse*, she's tipping the first of seven dominoes, setting into motion the steps that will produce all courses of a given meal. With an assist from the dining room team, who share the night's reservations with him

---

* Many restaurants have one or more quirks like this: For the entirety of its twenty-nine years, the influential American restaurant Chanterelle referred to *amuses* in the kitchen as "nuts" because a server in its first year was thrown by the kitchen's "giving away" little snacks at the start of a meal. "It's like when you go to a bar and get free nuts," explained the chef, David Waltuck—and a house tradition was born.

ahead of service, Thomas keeps a sheet taped to the tiled wall at his station that lists booking times and party sizes. This grants him a sort-of clairvoyance: He can see rushes before they come charging down the plain, and know in advance when a lull will free him up to clean and reset his station, or simply catch his breath and steal a swig from his water bottle, or run to the bathroom. (The sheet isn't common practice; rather, it's one of the idiosyncratic tricks a cook picks up or develops to help themself perform at their personal best.)

And so, the calling of the *amuse* is Thomas's starter pistol for each party's last three savory courses. Timing at Wherewithall is constant—for every meal I clocked while observing a week of service in July 2021, whether on a comparatively slow Tuesday or this bursting-at-the-seams Saturday, the snacks dropped approximately ten minutes after the server handed the corresponding chit off to the kitchen; and *Dry-Aged Strip Loin, Tomato, Sorrel*—the last savory course—arrived after almost exactly seventy-five minutes.

The first task Thomas performs in the preparation of our dish is removing enough portions of meat from the refrigerator to allow them to come to room temperature before cooking them. He removes portioned fish fillets at the same time, drizzles both with olive oil and seasons liberally with salt. Ensuring that these proteins aren't cold at the center sets the stage for success. Starting with a cold core all but guarantees overcooking. In the case of the meat, butchered into larger pieces that can toughen by the time the interior reaches its target temperature of 118°F, it also can result in an unpleasantly chewy exterior. The meat's doneness is monitored by an oven-probe thermometer plunged into its center; the thermometer's data, transmitted via a thread-thin wire, appears on a small, rectangular digital monitor that rests on the counter. Cooking beef—or any protein—expertly requires careful attention and a little faith: It must be tempered, then heated to something less than its desired final temperature and allowed to rest outside the oven so that carryover heat— the retained warmth that continues to cook it—can ease it to its target doneness. (Imagine a jet plane propelled by four engines for most of its journey, then shutting them off and gliding in for a landing.) The precious time when it's just right lasts for only a minute or two. One primary objective of the hot line, then, is to have it on the plate with the other elements, each at its desired temperature, ready to be whisked away to its destination table by a server within that time frame. It's not just ingredients that are brought to the right temperature: As courses near readiness, Reuben squats down to place the requisite number of plates or bowls into the lowboy oven beneath the stove, warming them before they receive their food. This sort of repetitive task can break a cook's body over time if they don't exercise, stretch, wear proper shoes, lift with their legs rather than their backs. (This is a far-off concern for Reuben, whose sinewy build and rubbery dexterity bring Spiderman to mind.) This week, warm bowls are needed for the oats; warm plates for the fish and meat. Earlier in the week, Reuben was warming them in stacks of three or four until Johnny, expediting momentarily, directed him to limit stacks to two plates or bowls, because the one(s) in the middle won't warm at the same rate. He and Thomas have since been warming plates not only in the low ovens but also under the salamander (the opensided broiler mounted to the wall above the stove) and, when no other options are available, on the counter using a handheld propane brûlée torch. The California chef David Kinch boils the craft of cooking down to the mastery of heat and evaporation, and that's sometimes true not just of food, but also of porcelain.

Among the prickly realities, like our own mortality, that our brains keep submerged beneath our consciousness to enable us to function, is that many of our most prized and delectable proteins come from animals. We know this but leave those dots unconnected so that we might savor a pristine fillet of Dover sole, a burnished roasted chicken, a sizzling strip steak, without guilt or queasiness. If you don't cook professionally, it's easy to hold the inconvenient truth about these foodstuffs at bay, because you only encounter them in their final form. Even most accomplished home cooks shop from bloodless cuts neatly aligned in a market's butcher case, rather than slaughter, or even break down, whole animals themselves.

These are my thoughts as I watch a worker on the kill floor of Slagel Family Farm, from which Where-withall purchases its strip loin, zap a lamb between the eyes with a two-pronged stunning rod, delivering an electric knockout punch that drops the beast to the concrete, senseless. The worker then curls a knife's edge around the animal's throat, penetrating the skin and releasing a glugging, crimson cataract powered by the animal's still-beating heart, quickening its demise. Next, the worker lifts the beast by one leg, drafting gravity to further hasten its death. It's undeniably grue-some, the dirty job that somebody must do. If you eat meat, you owe the people who do it a debt of gratitude. And it's nothing compared to what comes next: With the aid of a harness, what is now properly referred to as a carcass is hoisted up onto two cradles (sawhorses), a tube is inserted to the bottom of one leg where hoof meets shin, and air is pumped into the body, inflating it like a parade balloon to facilitate its flaying.

"If I made it this far, am I good?" I ask LouisJohn Slagel, my guide for the day. LouisJohn is the sly, thirty-something proprietor who helms the current iteration of Slagel Family Farm. Just before leading me from his butcher shop to the slaughterhouse, he had glanced over his shoulder and asked with a wicked grin, "You're not gonna pass out on me, are you?"

"I mean, I went to *cooking school*," I boasted, as macho as I could muster. "I've seen animals *butchered*."

Butchering, it turns out, is a Disney movie compared to this unceremonious snatching of life, the flaying of a fellow mammal, the stenchy eviction of organs that follows. (I had never considered the brilliant job flesh does to contain the sickening niff of organs, blood, and feces—the life-sustaining glop from which our brains would prefer to feign independence. The biological bouquet of that room haunted my olfactory senses for weeks.)

LouisJohn doesn't say any of that to me; instead, he just nods affirmatively. The gesture, though, is faintly marbled with bemusement, a discernible but plausibly deniable skepticism of this city slicker's delusion of fortitude.

We've spent about an hour together when the nod occurs. It required an email campaign, with an assist from Johnny and Beverly, to lock in an appointment with LouisJohn. This isn't uncommon with farm and food folk, who are chronically overworked and so understandably tend to zone out nonessential communication. I wrote again to confirm our appointment the night prior, and didn't receive his reply until I'd driven two hours south from Chicago, down I-294 to I-55, and finally along Illinois Route 47, which cuts a perfectly straight line through grassy farmland that extends to the horizon line on both sides until, suddenly, Route 47 passes through Forrest, where it briefly assumes the name *Center Street*. At the corner of Center and Krack, I turned into the parking area fronting a modest, old-fashioned strip mall, parked outside Slagel's butcher shop, and checked my email on my iPhone.

"Yes sounds good," read his response to the prior night's missive. "I'll probably smell like livestock though. Sorry." This was followed by a grimacing emoji.

As if on cue, the shop door opens and out strides a trim man in a black T-shirt. He closes the space between his shop and my car in what seems a nanosecond, his hand extended.

"LouisJohn," he says, as we shake, firmly. A smile forms above his black goatee.

Minutes later we're standing in the back room of his butcher shop, my pocket digital audio recorder on a stainless-steel worktable.

Like any proprietor who's welcomed enough journalists and customers to their establishments, LouisJohn
has his spiel down pat, and he launches right into it.

Slagel Family Farm is, relatively speaking, a small
family-owned concern located about one hundred miles
southwest of Chicago, in the Livingston County village
of Forrest, Illinois, population (in 2020) approximately
one thousand. According to the town's website, "Forrest was named in honor of a Mr. Forrest of New York
City, the business partner of Mr. Frost, President of the
T.P.W. Railroad at the time of incorporation in 1890."
The site features a one-man oral history of Forrest, told
by George Rex Clarke, an aged railway worker at the
time, to *The Forrest News*, and originally published in
print a half-century ago, on August 11, 1972.

Technically, Slagel Family Farm is the commercial
entity that processes and sells meat, poultry, and eggs—
almost exclusively to midwestern restaurants. If you've
ordered beef, pork, lamb, goat, chicken, duck, rabbit,
turkey, chicken eggs, or duck eggs at an eatery in the
Chicagoland area, odds are you've consumed a Slagel
product.

Casual observers and most customers take Slagel
Family Farm to be the entire operation, from farm to
slaughter to butchery and packing to a restaurant's delivery dock. In legal reality, the corporation buys livestock from a handful of independently owned family

farms, though all of them are Slagel (the extended family) owned. The family has produced five generations of farmers (and counting, presumably), and about half the clan—six households—is involved, with their homes and farms, usually on the same property, scattered amid the surrounding flatland.

If you're a metropolitan creature without the inclination or curiosity to have ventured much beyond your city's limits, know that the towns and villages within one hundred miles of your neighborhood Starbucks might be as countrified as that guest ranch you visited on vacation or the communities you learned about in that Steinbeck novel you read in high school. There are other differences: Chicago is as liberal as any American metropolis between the coasts; more than six months after the 2020 presidential election, Biden-Harris campaign posters still obscure shop doors and windows, and although there's currently no local mandate, many citizens choose to wear masks, even outdoors. In Forrest, scant public concessions to the pandemic are on display, and on some of the surrounding homesteads, front yard tributes to Donald Trump abide.

Forrest's town center is marked by the intersection of Center and Krack Streets. Center runs north–south; Krack, named for one of the town's earliest settlers, east–west. Slagel Family Farm, the public-facing part, is divided among three main facilities along Krack: a processing and packing facility on West Krack, a slaughterhouse on the other side of Center, and the Slagel butcher shop, Slagel Family Meats, which sits amid a strip of independent storefronts just a mile from where LouisJohn's great-great-grandfather settled in 1888. For most of the intervening 134 years, one or more Slagels has sold animals to large-scale meat purveyors like Excel Fresh Meats and Tyson Fresh Meats. That changed in the mid-aughts, when LouisJohn trained the company's sights on the restaurant industry, where he perceived an opportunity to market a product he believed to be superior.

LouisJohn traces his philosophy of raising meat to high school competitions he participated in as a member of the National FFA Organization, which, per its website, "prepares students for successful careers and a lifetime of informed choices in the global agriculture, food, fiber, and natural resources systems." (FFA originally stood for Future Farmers of America, but the initials were relieved of their meaning in 1988 to reflect its broadening mission.) The contests challenged students to identify fifty cuts of meat by sight alone, naming each one's species, wholesale cut, and retail cut, as well as multiple grades of the same cut from best (prime) to worst (canner). At Joliet Junior College, the nation's oldest public community college, LouisJohn studied ag production. The two-year program covered genetics, seeds, nutrition, and even made room for a primer on marketing. One exam tasked students with grading live animals the day before slaughter, then grading them in the cooler the next. The before-and-after exercise was an epiphany for LouisJohn: "All of that got me thinking that I'm not just raising animals," he says. "I'm raising *meat*. A lot of your livestock farmers are raising animals; that's the only way they think about it. I'm thinking of how the product *tastes* when we're done."

In the case of pork, for example, LouisJohn says: "My focus is how can I get hogs that are consistently good meat quality, good marbling, good PH,[*] consistency in texture." Slagels have been raising hogs for generations, so you might say that the overall operation runs on its own variation on the Darwinian edict: survival of the tastiest, with DNA that produces the most succulent hogs surviving the ages in gilts[†]—the porcine equivalent of a bread starter.

LouisJohn is the fourth oldest of thirteen siblings (six sisters and seven brothers, including him). Local tradition dictates that if a farm is viable at the time of one generation's retirement, the youngest son has first

---

[*] In meats and other foods, the PH level quantifies the amount of acidity, which impacts both flavor and the potential for growth of pathogenic bacteria.

[†] dedicated breeders

refusal on assuming control. LouisJohn's father had yet
to reach retirement age, and LouisJohn wasn't next in
the line of succession when he graduated in 2006.
Accordingly, he had two obvious options: seek out a full-
time non-Slagel job or expand the operation, generating
enough supplemental revenue to sustain his and possibly
a few siblings' families, perhaps by selecting a specific
breed, raising it in confinement farms, and creating a
factory. LouisJohn's father had taken over the business in
the 1970s and made minor tweaks, but had resisted converting to animal confinement, artificial insemination,
and other modern techniques that put a revenue-driven
emphasis on quantity over quality—and would have
compromised the farm's sterling reputation.

In a surprise move, in 2007, LouisJohn took over
his butcher shop from its prior owners. That transaction catalyzed Slagel Family Farm's transformation
to its current, primarily direct-to-restaurant iteration.
The store, previously known as Forrest Meats, sold to
locals, hardly a sufficient customer base to sustain itself,
never mind offering opportunity for growth. In 2008,
freshly married and ready to start a family, LouisJohn
hatched a plan to exponentially expand his clientele and
revenue by making Slagel a go-to supplier for big city
restaurants.

He took to *Chicago* magazine, yellow highlighter in
hand, and pored over the capsule restaurant reviews

in the back of the issue, coloring over any write-up featuring virtue-connoting buzzwords like *local*, *natural*, and/or *organic*. Then he cold-called them, pitching the farm's history and its intended transition, and requesting a meeting to introduce himself and drop off samples. A stranger to both the city and its chefs, LouisJohn hit paydirt on day one when he met Paul Kahan, the prolific Chicago chef-restaurateur behind One Off Hospitality Group and such local dining institutions as the French-inflected New American classic Blackbird in the West Loop (which closed in 2020), and the group's second effort, the wine-bar-turned-full-service-restaurant, avec. Timing was everything: Kahan planned to open his meat-orgy restaurant The Publican just a few months later.

"Within the next week we started bringing product in for tasting menus for The Publican. We've had a really good working relationship ever since," says LouisJohn.

Word of mouth spread, with some chefs purposefully connecting LouisJohn with colleagues who would help ensure the longevity of their new favorite meat supplier. Slagel swiftly spun a web of regional restaurant customers, concentrated in the Chicagoland area, with a smattering as far flung as St. Louis, Champaign, and Springfield.

Farmers can set goals, but opportunity just as often arises randomly, out of demand. When LouisJohn connected with Stephanie Izard, the season 4 *Top Chef* champ and chef of Chicago's Girl & the Goat restaurant and various spinoffs, all bearing hircine names, in Chicago and Los Angeles, she asked him if there were any cuts he needed to sell. (As with restaurants, less waste equals more profit for farms and ranches.) He'd been able to move pig cheeks but the business had been squandering significant quality yield from the heads. He quoted her a good price, and the dish she devised—*Wood Oven Roasted Pig Face*, for which the beast's visage is removed, seasoned with herbs, rolled, and braised, then sliced and cooked in a wood-burning oven—became an instant must-have and perennial best seller.

"If I run into somebody randomly and they've been to Girl & the Goat, most of them have had that dish," says LouisJohn. "And it was simply the result of, 'What do you want to get rid of?'"

Then there are the chain reactions, often resulting from a chef's inflated optimism. When Chicago's Nightwood restaurant shuttered, the chef, Jason Vincent, began planning his current hobbit hole–sized Logan Square hotspot, cheekily named Giant. On a tour of Slagel's operation, he told LouisJohn he intended to buy beef, pork, lamb, and eggs from him. He also asked him to start raising chickens, estimating he'd need about one hundred per week. It was found money: Unbeknownst to Vincent, Slagels had been raising chickens for their own personal consumption for years; now here was a turnkey opportunity for some of LouisJohn's younger siblings to earn income. The chef's estimate exceeded the emerging reality by forty chickens a week, which LouisJohn naturally offered to other chefs. In short order, the demand was up to one *thousand* chickens per week.

With so much livestock crisscrossing the area, it's difficult to quantify how many animals the Slagels cumulatively are raising at any time, but it can be estimated by extrapolating from how many they butcher each week. And so, for example, LouisJohn guesstimates that the thirty hogs butchered per week correlates to between one thousand and twelve hundred pigs, ranging from babies to breeding stock, in the family at any time.

"To put that in perspective, the guy down the road here has between five and ten *thousand* sows," says LouisJohn. (Farmers often have convenient counterpoints to their own practices a stone's throw away and just out of sight, dependably referred to as "this guy over here" or "that guy down there.") "I'm not saying there's anything wrong with what he's doing, but that's a *commercial* farm operation . . . it's a pretty big-scale

LouisJohn Slagel with members of his butchering and packing team

difference." That said, Slagel *is* big and nimble enough to accommodate a short-notice customer request in the hundreds of pounds.

Slagel's website lists more than one hundred businesses to which they sell. That network offers the Slagels fringe benefits. Increasingly, LouisJohn has found himself an invited guest at the full spectrum of ticketed and private "foodie" happenings. The exposure to conceptual multicourse bacchanals, friends-and-family* dress

---

* Friends-and-family dinners are practice services hosted by restaurants that can afford them. As the name suggests, intimates of the owner, operator, and chef dine free of charge, in exchange for feedback and a chance for the kitchen and dining room teams to identify any weaknesses before paying customers and critics descend.

rehearsals, and large-format meals rippled through his culinary life. As a result, when he takes to the kitchen at home, LouisJohn is apt to cook a restaurant-style dish out of one of the handful of cookbooks in his collection, like the duck with reduced jam sauce he'd made for his brother and sister-in-law a few nights before my visit, a far cry from the family meals of his childhood, larded with Americana classics like pot roast, baked potatoes, applesauce canned by his mother each autumn, and vegetables from the garden.

"I never dreamed of serving my family seared duck breast for Sunday dinner," says LouisJohn. "My wife says that we're food snobs now."

Back in May, the cow that yielded the strip loin for our dish at Wherewithall spent its days roaming freely between the shady confines of a red cattle barn outlined in white trim and the open-air lots, or pens, that flow into it. This specific farming operation is situated in front of the property LouisJohn bought in 2007, around the same time he took over the butcher shop. The house in which he lives with his wife and six young children is out back. Since then, he's rebuilt or replaced much of the farm structures and equipment that were in disuse by the former owners, whose children declined to inherit it. Here, as his siblings and other relatives do in the surrounding area, LouisJohn raises cattle, hogs, ducks, and laying hens. Walking the property—unusually muddy the day of my visit following a downpour the day prior—we're treated to a discordant symphony of animal utterances that would have made Old MacDonald feel right at home.

LouisJohn freely acknowledges that the scene here is a disconnect from the romanticized fantasy of modern-day progressive farming. The various components are strictly utilitarian, from the hay shed to the concrete feeder (a long, trough-like structure) to the feed shed. There's even a mountain of manure standing several feet high, unapologetically right out in the open.

Nor do the livestock roam endless acreage feeding on robust, verdant grass. Were LouisJohn based in, say, Ireland with its frequent rains and mild climate, he might raise grass-fed animals. But in southern Illinois, with its savagely hot, arid summers—on the day of my visit all of the cattle chose to laze in the relative cool of the shady barn—and subzero winters, they will be fed a diet of hay for half the year no matter what. And so LouisJohn feeds them a mixture of organic clover, oat straw, rye grass, and other grains grown and baled on his property. (He also disdains the wet quality of grass-fed beef, but that's another story.)

Caring for cattle at this scale is an easy lift; if not for his abundant business responsibilities, LouisJohn says he could tend to his livestock on his own. But since he's rarely on his farm during the workday, he employs one full-time worker who cares for and feeds them, and also repairs equipment and vehicles in the workshop on his premises. When reinforcements are called for, his mother, brother, and an occasional neighbor kid pitch in.

The more LouisJohn shares, the more his business instincts come into high relief: Roughly six years prior, he spearheaded the farm's taking the necessary steps to earn certified organic designation, not out of any high-minded sense of responsibility, but rather because of the increased revenue it promised. With the help of his brothers in the construction trade, he built an event space on his own property, got it licensed as a restaurant, and swiftly established it as a venue where Chicago-area chefs cook ticketed guest dinners using Slagel product. He's begun producing a line of pet food sold in frozen two-pound batches. Oh, and he bought the restaurant space next door to his production facility, initially just to avoid the possibility of conflict with a neighbor, but eventually opened a coffee and hamburger concept there—the coffee was shipped to him by his brother who works at an orphanage in Mexico, and the burgers were augmented with gourmet toppings. But the local clientele balked at shelling out $10 to $11 for a burger. Rather than compromise his standards and sensibility, he now rents the restaurant to the chef he used to employ.

Entrepreneurial acumen runs in the family. Louis-John estimates that within a twenty-five-mile radius, there are twenty-five businesses owned and operated by a Slagel, from a restaurant to a construction company to a cabinet shop to his own business. There's also a strong political gene: One of his cousins is the mayor and an uncle serves as school board president.

His ever-burgeoning enterprise is reflected in the unceasing flow of calls he fields as he makes his rounds. We'll have to take it on faith that the Bluetooth device hugging his left ear detaches at night. By day, they are inseparable. Everybody's looking for him—the office, his wife, and Chicago chefs and cooks, whose orders and modifications, even in the Internet Age, he often handles personally. He is manifestly a man of his environment, but his telecommunication habits would be right at home in the corridors of a Hollywood talent agency.

When the cattle have matured, they are transported by truck to the slaughtering facility's loading bay and gathered in a holding pen where they unknowingly await the prod. After the team on the kill floor—Ricky and Gerardo—stun, kill, bleed, and flay them, they are

After slaughter and butchery, the strip loin served in
our dish ages in this climate-controlled room.

hung on a gambrel fixed between their hind legs and
transported along a motorized processing line to the
evisceration room where they are gutted, then continue on their unmerry way to the scale room, where
they are weighed.

Also stationed in the scale room is a dedicated
USDA inspector, an employee of the United States
federal government, which assigns one to every meat
processing plant in the country. The inspector con-
trols access to a stamp that imprints the meat with
Slagel's five-digit inspection number, a requirement
for shipping anywhere in the nation. (The inspector

himself doesn't stamp the meat; rather, he grants the Slagel team access to the device for the time he's on the premises, and greenlights their stamping of each specimen.) By law, and at the business's expense, Slagel provides the inspector with an on-site office and a landline, and cannot process livestock in his absence. If the official's arrival is delayed for any reason—personal or professional—the slaughter crew must wait, accruing pay, until they materialize. (This sounds onerous, but in principle LouisJohn believes in the system as a deterrent for farms that might risk food safety in the absence of oversight. "Human nature is to cut corners," he says. "But you don't speed when there's a cop sitting there.")

Last comes the chill room, the coldest chamber in this facility, where the thermostat is set to 28°F. But owing to the animals' body heat and the constant opening and closing of the door, the temperature usually hovers between 32°F and 40°F. That's just above freezing, the intent being to extinguish body heat without producing ice crystals.

Carcasses generally remain in the chill room for one day, then are transported either to the original on-site butcher room (today used almost exclusively for custom processing for non-Slagel farms) or loaded onto a truck outfitted with rails and driven down the street to Slagel's butchering, aging, and packaging facility, built into a long-shuttered milk bottling plant that was "dilapidated and full of junk" when LouisJohn purchased it. The trucks back up to a loading dock, and the carcasses are unloaded.

Slagel's main processing room—about a block away on the other side of Forrest Street—is white, big and tall as a high school gymnasium, and noisy as hell. Amid a constant whirring of fans and buzzing of cutters, the high-ceilinged space houses various hubs: At any given time there are about fifteen workers packaging, filling orders, and grinding and making beef patties, often aided by machines designed for specific tasks (e.g., beef patty formers, vacuum sealers). There's also a long table on which animals are butchered by a team of about a half-dozen workers.

Beef, however, doesn't come directly here. Instead, it's quartered, then aged for up to three weeks in a carcass cooler before the quarters are butchered into individual cuts (sirloin, rib eye, strip loin, etc.) that are aged on steel utility shelving in a dedicated cooler for up to sixty days. This is where the strip loin in our dish would have spent its final two months.

Chefs order product from Slagel weekly. Orders are due on Sunday night, and LouisJohn will accept them through Monday. (Deadline flexibility is another commonality among people who do business with chefs.

Resistance to accommodate is futile.) He and his team gain a substantial head start by processing based on past ordering patterns, then making up any shortages by pulling more product from coolers or the field, if necessary. Conversely, if there's an excess, they'll include it in that week's CSA (community-supported agriculture) shipments, butcher it and sell the parts, or in the case of pork, use it in sausage, bratwurst, and other charcuterie.

Once it's packed, come Wednesday morning the meat is loaded onto trucks and delivered to restaurants, either by LouisJohn himself or one of two other drivers.

And now, here rest four ounces of Slagel meat, coming to the room temperature that will allow its being cooked to a precise doneness. After that's happened, Thomas will sear the beef on the plancha at his station, developing a light crust on both sides before transferring the piece to a steel tray, plunging the thermometer probe into its center, and sliding it into the oven. But for now, he has moved on to a quick-fire series of tasks, functioning on adrenaline and muscle memory at this point in the evening: He checks doneness of five portions of hake he's cooking in the oven, which in contrast to the meat are not judged with a thermometer but by how easily they flake apart (still a ways off). He consults with Reuben about the status of the appetizer course—a risotto-like oats preparation augmented by baby corn, baby chanterelles, bronze fennel, and a cured egg yolk. "Almost done," comes the answer as Reuben lines up six empty shallow bowls on the counter set just below the pass for the plate-up. He clarifies with Tayler the desired timing for having those five fish portions up. ("Five to seven minutes," she says.) Then he grabs one of the pots, which contains sautéed chanterelles, and follows Reuben, who's begun spooning oats into the bowls.

To produce the oats dish, Reuben has sautéed the chanterelles in butter in a small stainless-steel saucepan. In a separate saucepan, he has reheated the oats, which had been cooked, cooled, and stored prior to service. Into each bowl go the oats, followed by chanterelles. They're topped with crispy koji oats.* Then a house-cured egg yolk is transferred from the salt-sugar brine in which it's held in a deep Lexan to the center of the bowl with a slotted spoon, followed by a scattering of raw baby corn that's been sliced crosswise into thin coins, and bronze fennel, an herb that in appear-

---

* a traditional Japanese curing and flavoring agent, usually inoculated into cooked grains

Jenna Cole, the most junior member of the
Wherewithall kitchen team, prepares crudité.

ance resembles dill but delivers the licorice punch of
its namesake. Over the course of the week, the team
has gone from contributing to each bowl with no individual ownership of specific tasks to—at Johnny's
direction—each team member doing one task across
all the bowls for each plate-up, to help consistency and
ensure that every component finds its way into each
serving. So Reuben spoons in the oats; Thomas follows
with the chanterelles; Reuben trades his saucepan for
the container holding the koji and adds that, and so
on. Somewhere along the way, Tayler perceives a discrepancy in the concentration of chanterelles among

the bowls, leans forward over the counter, and plucks one from an especially dense portion with long steel tweezers, relocating it to another serving.*

Meantime, Jenna has started plating the snacks for Table 12. When she notices the eruption of action she steps to the hot line to pitch in, picking up a small rectangular tray of bronze fennel atop an open paper towel (there to absorb any moisture) and arranging fronds over oats compositions as they're otherwise completed. Jenna's not a member of the hot line, but intermittently contributing like this saves her colleagues seconds that add up to potentially lifesaving *minutes* over the course of a busy service. As her own workflow allows, she will finish the fish dish with sea beans, or set sorrel leaves atop the strip loin on the meat course, or ladle sauce from small pots onto either of those compositions.

Jenna's the house hotshot, the Wherewithall wunderkind. If they're lucky, every kitchen has one: a young, malleable cook with natural aptitude, a sunny attitude, and a soldier's work ethic, whom everyone knows is going places. It's an especially good person to be in a restaurant kitchen, where the possibility of advance-

---

* If you've never seen Martin Scorsese's *Casino*, there's a blueberry muffin scene that will now ring extra true when you do.

ment is as omnipresent as the scent of wine reducing. This is all the more true in the wake of the employee exodus (nicknamed "The Great Resignation") that followed the worst of COVID, which prompted many workers in a variety of industries to reevaluate their career and life choices. Because professional cooking demands long hours—including nights, weekends, and holidays—for paltry pay and few, if any, benefits, this societal shift sent an especially disruptive shockwave through restaurants. If you possess soft hands, the multitasking gene, and desire, chances are you'll be ascending the house hierarchy just as soon as that cook on the next rung no-shows because they took another job, or lights out for a *stage** in Copenhagen, or crawls out of a bottle and into rehab, or wakes up one day relieved of the illusion that this life is sustainable and is off somewhere dabbling in domesticity and studying for their real estate license exam.

Just a few years ago, Jenna was a go-getting high schooler in Danville, a small Pennsylvania town, about 150 miles northwest of Philadelphia. In Montour County, which has a roughly 10 percent poverty rate, Danville boasts an enviable economy centered on Geisinger Medical Center, a sprawling hospital complex

---

* a short-term cooking job, often for no pay, forgone in exchange for knowledge, contacts, and references; the term is an Americanization of the French word *stagiaire*, which refers to the person working in the position

of mismatched architectural styles that's endured and expanded over more than a century. A *Sliding Doors* version of Jenna's life played on an endless loop a few boroughs over in Centralia, which has long been a history buff's treasure trove for entirely tragic reasons: A 1962 mine fire of indeterminate origin wasn't properly contained; it continues to smolder underground to this day, rendering the area uninhabitable. The local zip code was eighty-sixed in 2002, and the 2020 census accounted for a mere *five* holdout residents. The deserted streets were a skateboarder's paradise, attracting Jenna and fellow thrashers; the macadam, softened by years of slow roasting from below, sometimes buckled underwheel.

Jenna and her younger brother were fortunate to be born to self-employed parents largely immune to the local roller-coaster economy: Her father is an owner of Cole's Hardware, a family business for four generations that has expanded to thirteen locations shared by her father and uncle. Jenna's mother, a child psychologist who occasionally treats adults, was once on staff at Geisinger and now operates a private practice. In an area beset by destitution and its attendant issues, her business is grimly brisk.

Jenna was a solid student and sufficiently adept at speech and debate that she participated in state and national contests. She was also an avid musician, playing bassoon in honors band and competitions. In the sports realm, she relished the "mental chess" and self-reliance of fencing so much that she might someday pick it up again, but in team sports like lacrosse and soccer she considered herself a drag on her teammates.

Even in this era of culinary celebrity, most professional cooks meander into their careers, usually trying one or more conservative paths before discovering or committing to the kitchen. Almost to a person, there exists what might be called "the portal"—the first gig of dishwashing, prepping ingredients, or maybe waiting tables in the dining room—that activated the cook within and supplied that ultimately addictive first taste of restaurant life, whether they surrendered to it immediately or postponed the inevitable. For Jenna, the portal was a high school job at Brews N Bytes Internet Cafe & Eatery. As "Bytes" implies, the restaurant offered Wi-Fi, but the name was otherwise a misnomer, promising pub grub but instead serving Cuban and Dominican staples that reflect the owners' heritage. This was unusual in Danville, as was the background of their baker, raised in Barcelona and trained in the European ways. Jenna started as a barista and waitress, and in time, prompted as much by hunger as anything else, began helping in the kitchen. This led to catering gigs with the family and pitching in day to day in the two-person kitchen when they needed an extra pair of hands, even just for rudimentary tasks like slicing lettuce and tomatoes for sandwiches and salads.

Food wasn't a preoccupation, but Jenna thirsted for travel, bingeing the Anthony Bourdain series *No Reservations* on sick days, and one year convincing her family to shell out for a vacation in Belize. And so, a happy byproduct of working at Brews N Bytes was traveling via her palate, snacking on empanadas and pastelitos (small, flaky filled pastries). Jenna disdained small-town life, despite the relative comfort of her circumstances. She craved big-city action and anonymity, and saw music as a bridge because most prominent music schools are situated in major cities. Specifically, Chicago had been on her mind since she'd visited for a national high school speech and debate competition. She chose DePaul University School of Music, in the city's Lincoln Park neighborhood, in pursuit of a degree in classical performance. While there, an accident ended her commitment to skateboarding while simultaneously signaling her then-latent pro-kitchen constitution: Skating with her bassoon case in tow, she lost her balance and fell, her wrist catching the brunt of the impact. She managed to scribble an essay in class before dashing off to the emergency room, and toughed it out through a rehearsal later that same day, her hand swollen and throbbing.

Chicago offered abundant opportunities to sensorially satisfy her wanderlust with food, chowing down in Chinatown and at the concentration of Vietnamese restaurants on Argyle Street, or brewing Thai iced tea at home and snacking from ten-pound bags of Chinese candies purchased during her walkarounds.

Culinary awakening coincided with music fatigue. Ten-hour practices had exhausted their novelty, and on completing her sophomore year, Jenna admitted to herself that she was terminally burnt out. She withdrew from the program and hasn't unclasped her bassoon case since. The ensuing, unfamiliar aimlessness irritated this born striver. In swooped a friend, a fellow music school dropout who'd attended Chicago's Kendall College's culinary school—the American Midwest's preeminent cooking school—and inspired her to interview there. Within two months, she had matriculated. College credits sped her toward a degree, enabling her to complete the two-year program in one year. She enjoyed cooking school from the get-go, despite her relative inexperience. To catch up with her classmates, she sharpened her knife skills at home nightly, perfecting various cuts on onions and potatoes. "I went through so many potatoes," she laughs, "that I started making potato doughnuts for my roommates." She also availed herself of the school's free tutoring program in which she performed basic kitchen tasks as an instructor observed, coached, and corrected her. This brought about an epiphany regarding her relationship to music versus cooking: Both require an aptitude and capacity for repetitive tasks, but the solitude and exacting nature of music taxed her whereas the more forgiving, correctable, and social nature of cooking energized her.

After a year (less in Jenna's case), with the goal of folding practical experience into their education, Kendall requires its students to spend several months externing at a restaurant. Following her innate wanderlust, Jenna landed a coveted externship at Angle (pronounced ANH-glay), a modernist cuisine restaurant in Barcelona that possessed one Michelin star when she arrived in August 2019, and two stars three months later, when she left.

She describes her time in Spain as "probably the hardest thing I've ever done in my life," beginning with a not-uncommon rite of passage for an American whisk overseas: Navigating from the local (in this case, Barcelona) airport to her place of employment tested her improvisational skills and moxie. Her passable Spanish, earned in AP classes in high school and on the job at Brews N Bytes, didn't provide the leg up she thought it would in a Catalan-speaking province. One wrong train and many hours later, she washed up at Angle, where the house patois was an ever-shifting mashup of Spanish and Catalan, seasoned with a complement of words from other languages (mostly Portuguese and Peruvian Spanish) based on who was working there at the time. Her worldly co-workers effortlessly surfed the linguistic wave, but she was lost, and her Spanish deteriorated due to her inability to disentangle so many words that sounded similar to her American ear.

As do other restaurants dependent in part on free labor, Angle provided no-frills housing for interns and *stages*, a villa adjacent to the owners' other restaurant, the Michelin two-star ABaC. Four young women—all the others Spanish speakers—slept in two bunkbeds in a dorm room–sized space bereft of air conditioning or artificial heat. (This surprised Jenna; extrapolating from the restaurant's hotel address, she'd assumed a guest room awaited her.) Her kitchen orientation was no more comfortable: The woman she'd be replacing was set to depart just a day after Jenna's arrival, so following a crash course in garde manger, she was tossed into the salad bowl, working service in a foreign land. Like Wherewithall, the restaurant operated according to old-school European structure: Cooks spent the day prepping the ingredients they themselves would be cooking, combining, and/or plating at night, then worked service. Jenna started her day at ten-thirty in the morning, worked until three in the afternoon, took a siesta, and returned for dinner service, cooking and then cleaning the kitchen until after midnight.

It was sink or swim; after about a month Jenna swam, thanks in part to her personal lifeguard—a kindly pastry chef who'd picked up English during a kitchen stint in Miami, Florida. Jenna acclimated to the staff's quirky lingo and became proficient in the basic techniques required to produce menu items like a green gazpacho ice cream, made in small batches throughout service, which called for the application of liquid nitrogen, and spherifying elements like black garlic puree.[*]

During her short tenure, Jenna developed an appreciation for sublime fish and shellfish, like oysters and brilliant crimson carabinero prawns, still beaded with the water from which they were harvested. But when her three months were up, she evaluated her relationship with modernist cuisine thusly: "I'm very glad I did it, and I learned a lot about that. But it wasn't my thing."

She returned to Chicago that December, and after a brief job search started working at Parachute in late February 2020, just three weeks before COVID-19 forced its temporary closure. After helping out sporadically at

---

[*] These techniques and methods were popularized by Spanish chef Ferran Adrià, modernist cuisine's papa, at his storied, now-shuttered restaurant El Bulli, about a two-hour drive up the coastline from Angle.

Little Parachute (the adaptive, take-out iteration of the restaurant with relatively traditional Korean offerings such as bibimbap and rice bowls) and at Wherewithall in fits and starts, she joined the team when the restaurant reopened for indoor dining in June 2021.

And now here she is, a few weeks later, scattering that bronze fennel over the oats dish.

Thomas and Reuben swiftly move the finished dishes from the counter up onto the pass; across from them, José, Carly Phillips, one of the servers, and Griffin Bulger, a server assistant, stand waiting, hands at the ready.

"Four of these are for Table 2," Tayler tells José, completing the X on that table's appetizer course box. "And two are for Table 9," she says to Carly, finishing that one's X. José and Griffin each pick up two bowls and Griffin follows José to his table. Carly picks up her cargo and flies away toward hers.

Jenna returns to her station and resumes plating Table 12's crudité, which she'd been working on a minute ago. "Here we get super farm-fresh vegetables," she says matter-of-factly as I observe, imagining her as a chef in the future, speaking to some other journalist in her own restaurant. "And I think that's what makes a great crudité great."

The freshness demands flexibility; in this case, the composition of the plate has changed over the week—early on, there were farm-apple wedges, but the supply is almost depleted so, tonight, it's orange and purple cauliflower, orange and purple carrots, and lemon cucumbers. Jenna spritzes them all with a mist of olive oil mixed with rosé vinegar, and arranges them on a small plate, into the center of which she's spooned a goat's-milk yogurt aioli (the house name for an emulsion of equal parts yogurt and aioli made with roasted garlic) and a brilliant green nasturtium oil.

The crudité is one of two snacks tonight; the other is a marinated mussel "wrap"—a DIY affair for the guests who are presented with a small plate arrayed with chilled marinated, shelled mussels, julienned raw kohlrabi, herbs, and shiso leaves. (Guests will be advised by their server to arrange the mussels, kohlrabi, and herbs atop the shiso, then pick it up and eat it like a taco.)

At roughly 8:20 P.M., Jenna puts Table 12's crudité up on the pass.

Wherewithall doesn't list the snacks, broth, or bread and butter on the menu; Beverly and Johnny prefer them to be surprising—for first timers, anyway—and value additive, a little something extra from the kitchen.

2

Menu Meeting

Nooshâ delivers the crudité to Table 12, briefly delineating the vegetables and condiments for the guests. Next will come the mussel wraps, and then the broth, served with the bread and butter. The first dish promised by the printed menu—the appetizer course of oats "risotto"*— won't arrive for about twenty-five minutes.

The first stirrings of a given week's menu at Wherewithall come about the week prior, usually in the wee small hours after service on Thursday night, or Friday morning if you want to be technical about it. Johnny and Tayler sit across from each other at one of the small, round cafe tables in the courtyard behind the bar and, over a glass of wine, review what product will

---

* *Risotto* technically refers to a rice dish. The quotation marks here indicate that another grain is being treated in a risotto-like way.

be left in-house after the present week, and what the restaurant's preferred farms have made available for the following week. From there, the chefs bat around ideas for dishes, and a *progression* of dishes, some of which will be tested and course corrected on Friday and Saturday, after which orders will be placed for the necessary ingredients.

Let's wind back to two nights ago, after Thursday's dinner service. The time is 12:30 on Friday morning. Inside Wherewithall, the dishwashers wrap up their work and cooks scrub down the kitchen. Out back, in the courtyard, Johnny waits for Tayler to join him to brainstorm the following week's menu. The summer air around us is still, a playlist of country music wafting softly from an outdoor speaker. Johnny sips a glass of red Zweigelt from the Austrian producer Arndorfer, owned and operated by the husband-and-wife team of Martin Arndorfer and Anna (Steininger) Arndorfer. The bottle, with red script on a white label, rests on the table.

"Ideas for dishes come from everywhere," Johnny tells me. Case in point: a memory that, apropos nothing, surfaced for Beverly as she and Johnny walked François in mid-July sparked this week's strip loin composition. The memory was a go-to duo that had been in rotation in an old catering job: slices of tender, rosy-rare roasted beef tenderloin over roasted cherry

Johnny and Tayler brainstorm the following week's menu.

tomatoes that had been tossed with their own juices and balsamic vinegar, and strewn with minced fresh herbs. This in turn activated Johnny's recollection of a modern variation on the same theme that he encountered in an early kitchen gig, from which he plucked the idea of dehydrating the tomatoes. From that spontaneous exchange, the framework of this week's final savory course had been established.

Tayler emerges from the barroom cupping a wine glass, her body slack and tension-free now that service is done. She joins us, filling the glass with Zweigelt as Johnny rhapsodizes about the elemental pleasures of beef: "I love rich beef with acid," he says, tilting his head back to gaze up between the buildings at the night sky and its smattering of stars. "I don't like to eat protein with tons of different stuff. I like it very simple."[*]

Tayler recounts the trial and error that resulted in the treatment of the tomato in this week's meat course: Sitting in the same spot a week prior, she'd suggested brining them in an umami solution, but that rendered the tomatoes soggy, even after a trial turn in the oven. Ultimately, simply dehydrating unadorned tomatoes achieved the desired concentrated flavor without what Tayler describes as "a Sunday gravy quality." On Tuesday, without the benefit of an overnight sauna (the restaurant is closed on Mondays), Tayler peeled the tomatoes to expose their flesh and speed the process, then cut them in half to put the gooey locules in direct contact with the heat. This saved time, but in truth guests who ate the dish from Wednesday onward feasted on a slightly less hydrated tomato than did those on Tuesday.

Tayler's still in the nascency of her tenure at Wherewithall because it's only been reopened as a full-service restaurant for a month. Moreover, chef de cuisine is a new position at Wherewithall that didn't exist there pre-pandemic. It's been added by Beverly and

---

[*] This is somewhat unusual outside a steakhouse. Most chefs who turn out expressive cuisine don't enjoy devising beef main courses, because the beef dominates any plate, limiting the possibilities.

Johnny to help free up their time for parenthood and other business and altruistic obligations and pursuits. Tayler shares creative duties with them and stewards the operation from day to day and during service. In time, Johnny and Beverly will let the rope out, and Tayler, who had only eaten at the restaurant once before accepting the job, will function more autonomously, setting the menu herself. At least that's the plan—the chemistry of this trio and the greater restaurant team will emerge over time, as it must.

"It feels like a whole new opening," says Johnny. "We're still establishing the vision of the restaurant."

If Parachute and Wherewithall are children of a sort of Beverly and Johnny, Parachute favors her while Wherewithall more resembles him, especially in the influence of Le Châteaubriand, a Parisian restaurant at which he *staged* several years ago (more on this in a bit). And so Beverly influences the menu, but it's Johnny who confers with Tayler in the Thursday night ideation sessions. Fortunately, they have compatible food mindsets, driven in part by humility; neither desires to show off on the plate.

"The best things happen by chance," he says. "We're not trying to blow people's minds here, and not trying to blow our own minds, either. If we just do what tastes good, those other fun things that come out of nowhere will just appear." That said, Johnny confesses that he sometimes has to stifle an urge to assuage his own insecurities by taking big swings. "I need to be less hard on myself and not put so much pressure on myself," he says.

With that, Johnny and Tayler launch into their first ideation session for next week's menu. In the breathlessness of the restaurant's busiest week in more than a year, Tayler has scarcely found time to think about life beyond Saturday night. But she does have one idea for the next menu, for the intermezzo (pre-dessert), and with it this week's dialogue begins:

TAYLER
Butternut Sustainable Farm will have its first Sungold tomatoes of the season in next week. *They're so sweet and good.* I was thinking of doing a tomato sorbet or granita with them.

JOHNNY
What if it was that bridge of savory and sweet? Maybe use goat cottage cheese with tomato sorbet.

TAYLER
I think that'd be delicious. Lightly sweeten the goat cottage cheese.

Thomas sticks his head out from the barroom.

THOMAS
Any thoughts about staff meal for tomorrow?

TAYLER
You should definitely use up the beef and cod.*

JOHNNY
You can set up two hotel pans and just steam
the cod.

Thomas nods and reenters the restaurant.

TAYLER
I've been kind of wanting to do something similar
to what I've been doing for the tasting: Feuille de
brick that we toasted—

JOHNNY
Is that too labor intensive?

TAYLER
I think it'd be fun and tasty and different, like a
flour tortilla vibe—

JOHNNY
It could be a little thicker.

---

* Cod was used in the fish course through Friday, then replaced with hake.

TAYLER

I was thinking more crepe-y. Or we could do strips of it and roll it. If we have any fish left over, we could make a rillette and smoke it Saturday and roll the fish in it. We can put pans on that burner and cook them to order.

JOHNNY

Maybe greens, or *bitter* greens?

TAYLER

Or mustards—

JOHNNY

We need to think it through a little, but we have the vessel.

Tayler moves on to another dish.

TAYLER

We mentioned doing a radish broth and they're here. If I start it tomorrow do you think it'll be—

JOHNNY

I think we should shoot for it and have another plan if it's not ready. Use that recipe for water kimchi, and double it.

TAYLER

We have twenty pounds in; I can order more.

JOHNNY

What's the other snack?

TAYLER

We can do crudité again. I love crudité. Our snacks are often fried, but in the summer—

JOHNNY

What if we keep changing it up, use different vegetables?

TAYLER
(*nods affirmatively*)

There's stuff down there; we don't need to order anything.

Abbie Rhoads, one of the bartenders, sticks her head out from the barroom.

ABBIE

Goodnight, guys!

JOHNNY AND TAYLER

Goodnight, Abbie!

Johnny SIGHS, SMILES, looks up at the stars.

> JOHNNY
> (*musing*)
> These weekly menus . . . it takes the younger cooks a little while to get it, but when they do, they become useful. They get used to versatility. They're not like robots. They get, like, years of experience in a few weeks.

He snaps out of his reverie; returns his attention to Tayler and the task at hand.

> JOHNNY
> What's an appetizer where we can really highlight the produce? We're at the peak of summer right now.

Tayler rummages through the papers fastened to her clipboard, stops on a list from Nichols Farm & Orchard.

> TAYLER
> Peppers. Fennel is coming up. Beets would be nice.
> (*beat*)
> Corn.

> JOHNNY
> I like that appetizer situation where you can just warm it up. People love it and it keeps service so

smooth. We have all those beans. We wanted to use some [on the small-plates menu offered] at the bar, but we don't have to; we can freeze them and do a bell pepper–focused bean dish.

TAYLER

All the peppers are blowing up right now. I keep looking for Jimmy Nardellos. And kale, dandelion greens. I know you don't necessarily like them but—

JOHNNY

I don't have anything against them; I just haven't figured out how to use them yet.

TAYLER

Swiss chard?

JOHNNY

Lots of wax beans and stuff. Stewed wax beans are *so* good. I have this weird guilty pleasure of eating canned beans.

TAYLER
(scrunches her face)

Gross! I never had canned vegetables as a kid.

JOHNNY

I like the texture. I always buy fresh green beans, but I like that texture where it's braised down;

my grandmother put a ham hock in a Crock-Pot
and tons of beans and just cooked it.

TAYLER
They do that in barbecue places—

JOHNNY
—with pan broth or something.

TAYLER
(chuckles)
We used to make a black garlic and ham hock
broth at Blackbird when I was really young.
You'd get in trouble when you opened the pressure cooker because it smelled like farts. One
time, a lunch cook did that right at the beginning
of dinner service . . . not good.

Johnny cracks up, then bursts forth with an idea.

JOHNNY
What if we make it like dashi,* with katsuo-
bushi,† and use tuna floss as the ham? Did you
try the tuna floss?

Tayler shakes her head "no."

---

* Japanese soup stock

† bonito flakes

TAYLER

I have to blend it; it's dehydrated.

JOHNNY

That'd be good, too, because it's pescatarian.

TAYLER

We smoked it before we dehydrated it.

JOHNNY

Oh, that's perfect. I think maybe we're onto something with that one.

TAYLER

I can make a batch of broth tomorrow and try it out.

JOHNNY
(trying out a name for the dish)

Basque.
    (beat)
Tuna.
    (beat)
Stew.
    (beat)
Something in that vein. We could even put some of those Basque pickled chiles on there.

Tayler suggests mackerel for the fish course, but Johnny worries that with the tuna in place, it's too much oily fish for one menu. He suggests white-fleshed fluke or halibut. Tayler volunteers that halibut is currently selling for a modest price.

All this fish talk prompts a conversation about halibut. Tayler's favorite way to cook it is by searing it in butter, then flipping it, removing it from the heat, and letting the other side poach in the still-hot fat. Johnny's favorite halibut dish was by chef Rafael Lunetta at a restaurant called JiRaffe in Santa Monica, California. He ate it twenty-one years ago but can still see and taste it: baked in a little crock with broth, new potatoes, and olive oil, and capped with puff pastry to trap and intensify the juices.

Suddenly, the floodgates open and Johnny and Tayler free-associate, rapid-fire.

TAYLER
What's the filo pastry that's like the little—

JOHNNY
Kataifi?* That'd be cool. Bake it—

TAYLER
—and Swiss chard—

---

* shredded filo dough

JOHNNY

Take it in that Greek-ish direction with lots of olive oil, maybe cured olives for a pop of salt.

TAYLER

When I was in Greece, they always did steamed mussels in tomato broth with little chunks of feta for bursts of salt.

JOHNNY
(makes a "whoa, Nelly" gesture)
We don't want to *overdo* it, either.

TAYLER

What if we didn't do olives but instead capers or caper leaves, spread under the fish?

JOHNNY

I almost think something like Swiss chard, chopped up, mixed into an aioli gribiche: lots of chopped Swiss chard, quickly sautéed, mixed into mayo with capers and egg, maybe a little mustard. I picture those textures really being highlighted: the fish, toasty and crunchy, and then something to make it all stick together when you eat it—

TAYLER

—almost like Basque spanakopita.

JOHNNY

Yeah, maybe we think of it like that.

TAYLER

Maybe we do a feta aioli, like a tartar sauce.

JOHNNY

The one thing I worry about is overpowering the halibut; we have to be careful.

The fish dish sufficiently on its way, they move on to the meat course, which at Wherewithall could be centered on poultry.

TAYLER

What if we did duck breast?

Perhaps. But any fiscally mature restaurant strives for phantom frugality.

JOHNNY

Do you think we're going to have leftover beef?

TAYLER

I don't think so and if we do, not that much.

JOHNNY

If we have these proteins left over, we should plan on making a snack with them for two days. At Le Châteaubriand, nothing got wasted; it all got turned into a snack. If they had fish, they'd make a rillette; if they had beef, they'd make a tartare. We should do that, even if it's just for one day. That's also good if we ever have a person come in twice in one week.*

They brainstorm about ducks: the relative merits of muscovy (gamey), Rohan (lots of delicious fat), moulard, and magret. They briefly consider serving quail or squab, but those are too pricey to fit Where-withall's food-cost model.

JOHNNY

I always hit a wall right here. The ideas are spinning and I get to the meat part and it's like—

TAYLER

Meat to me always feels boring almost. I like more vegetables or fish; personally that's what I want to eat.

JOHNNY

That's why I sometimes make just meat with a condiment.

TAYLER

Maybe with some kind of root, or fennel or something?

---

* In case it's not obvious, he means that a returning guest likely will not be served the same snack twice within the same week.

> JOHNNY

Broccoli's in season.

> TAYLER

Duck with broccoli and a ton of herbs?

> JOHNNY
> *(sighs)*

It's always going to come down to Tuesday. I want to commit to ordering these things and then figure it out. Put ourselves under the gun.

> TAYLER

I think the halibut will be good. The tomato pre-dessert, I feel confident about that. For dessert, I'm thinking something classic: sweet corn and blueberries.

> JOHNNY
> *(nods)*

The rest will unfold over the next few days.

It's nearly two A.M. They stand and walk into the empty restaurant, leave their wine glasses on the bar, and exit onto North Elston, locking the door behind them.

The team who arrive for work at eleven A.M. each Tuesday are a quartet in transition from their civilian

The kitchen team begin their week on Tuesday, as
Tayler downloads the menu to them.

selves to their kitchen alter-egos. They also person-
ify an industry sea change from the prior century's
hard-partying cooks to something less self-abusive.
They don't haul their bloated corpses into the kitchen,
trading ribald, liquor-drenched weekend war stories.
(Some also demonstrate the contemporary cook's love
of body art. There are tattoos of elephants, flowers,
daggers, and abstract shapes—some in isolation, others
packed tightly together into limb-covering sleeves.)
Instead, they're pink-cheeked and alert, with a skip
in their step and updates as wholesome as their com-
plexions. Mindful of hydration, a couple of them sip

from water bottles, and it wouldn't read the least bit incongruous if one had a rolled yoga mat tucked under-arm. We're there with them now, this past Tuesday as the menu being served this week was conveyed. As Tayler takes inverted chairs down from Table 10, the one closest to the kitchen, Reuben relates his visit to a waterpark. Tayler and Reuben slide into the banquette, leaving Thomas and Jenna the chairs. The cooks set their blue Bragard aprons, rolled and tied with their strings, on the table. Jenna shares that she saw the just-released Nicolas Cage vehicle *Pig*, a surprise critical hit in which the gonzo actor goes sub rosa as a reclusive ex-chef on a mission to root out the abductors of his only companion—a truffle pig with whom he shared a Robinson Crusoe existence in the woods outside Port-land, Oregon. Perhaps best of all, after more than a year of COVID, she saw it *in a theater*.

"I thought it would be stupid," Jenna says. "And then . . . I'm *crying*." She catches her head in her hands and laughs at the notion of sobbing at a movie about Nicolas Cage's devotion to a pig.

The first order of business at the start of the week is downloading the menu to the team, which is why they report for duty at eleven on Tuesdays and noon the rest of the week. Other than Tayler, who co-conceived it with Johnny in a session like the one we observed, nobody knows much, if anything, about what's coming.

But if there's one certainty this summer day, it's that by six P.M., they'll have cooked, refined, and started serving all seven courses to paying customers.

Tayler begins: Like last week, one of the snacks will be crudité. There's a surplus of wax and green beans that will be used, complemented by orange cauliflower and recently arrived romanesco. There are also baby carrots that, per Johnny, might find their way onto the meat course or possibly dessert. (Stay flexible, Tayler advises.) The crudité will be served with two dippings: a goat's-milk yogurt aioli (the aforementioned yogurt-aioli emulsion) and a nasturtium pesto, a spin on the popular Ligurian green sauce usually made with basil; this version also substitutes sunflower seeds for pine nuts to bypass any nut allergies, one fewer possible modification to contend with in the crossfire hurricane of service. And here's that phantom frugality: Pesto is traditionally made with Parmigiano-Reggiano, but there's leftover Manchego (a Spanish sheep's-milk cheese) left in the walk-in,* so Tayler advises Jenna to use that. The other snack will be marinated mussels with raw kohlrabi, set on a shiso leaf, along with yet-to-be-determined herbs.

The broth this week, Tayler informs the team, will be a heavily seasoned beef broth, with the caramelized

---

* pro kitchen shorthand for "walk-in refrigerator"

oomph of a French onion soup, but clarified. The broth
will be made with thyme, garlic, super slowly caramelized
onions, and a deglazing of sherry. The base stock will be
chicken, with roasted beef scrap and beef bones added to
impart their flavor, then strained out. (A caramelized onion stock with vegetable stock in place of chicken will be
prepared for any noncarnivorous guests.)

The appetizer course, Tayler explains, "will be whole
oats from Three Sisters Garden," a small family farm
roughly sixty miles south of Wherewithall, in Kankakee,
Illinois.

"It's going to be like a risotto," she tells Reuben,
who will make a reality of her words; he perks up and
scribbles in his small steno pad.

"There's going to be button chanterelles, shaved baby
corn, cured egg yolk, and then I made koji out of the
same oats, so we're going to do crispy koji oats on there
as well. And it will be finished with bronze fennel."

Making risotto is a rudimentary task familiar to
any line cook worth their salt, so Tayler confines her
instruction to this one's distinguishing characteristics:
The baby corn will yield an embarrassment of husks, so
Tayler instructs Reuben to reserve some and add them
to the vegetable stock for the "risotto." This will imbue
the oats with a corn flavor that, like Lebowski's* rug did

* Sorry. The Dude's.

his living room, will tie the dish together. Tayler also cautions Reuben that the most high-maintenance element of the dish is the one that might seem most turnkey: the cured egg yolk. Firstly, yolks need to be gently separated from whites, lest they break. They will be quick-cured in a salt-sugar brine in batches starting just before service, and as necessary throughout the night, because if left in the cure too long, the yolks will develop an unappealing "skin," over-cure, and dry out, or break.

Because the oat "risotto" will be topped with a cured egg yolk, there will be a glut of egg whites in-house. These will be used to clarify the broth—the textbook method for making consommé in which whites congeal into a meringue-like raft that floats on its surface, drawing impurities from the liquid.

The professional kitchen hierarchy—traditionally referred to in the Western world as a *brigade*—was modeled on the military: *chef*, for example, means *chief*. Many vestiges of that orientation remain, even in kinder, gentler kitchens like Wherewithall's. The call-and-response between Tayler and Jenna during service echoes the cadence of an order and the affirmation that acknowledge its receipt. This verges on the baroque, but sitting here at the beginning of the week, it does feel like a mission, or a heist, is being planned.

"On to the fish course," says Tayler, prompting Thomas to redouble his engagement and ready his pen as well. (Technically, Reuben serves as *entremetier,* or fish cook, and Thomas as *viand,* or meat cook, but as it's just the two of them on the hot line, both need to be able to make both courses. That said, responsibility for the appetizer rests with Reuben.) Hake will be gently poached in olive oil and served with the little heads of gem lettuce expected from Nichols Farm & Orchard, which will be braised to order, Tayler informs them. The dish will be blanketed by a sauce of vin jaune, a fortified white wine from France's Jura region, and butter, and topped with naturally salty green sea beans, which resemble miniature asparagus. Hake and cod are similar fish—white fleshed, with a large flake—and there's some hake in the house, so that will be used on Tuesday, then cod, and then hake again after a fresh delivery arrives at week's end, by which time the cod should be depleted.

Throughout the meeting, the restaurant comes alive around the team. General manager Jessica arrives and settles in by snipping and pulling dead leaves and whatnot from the little plants arranged around the dining room. Delivery men from various farms and purveyors arrive with items Tayler has been expecting: Regalis Foods, a seller of luxury ingredients, drops off chanterelle mushrooms and sea beans; Fortune Fish & Gourmet leaves samples of hake their sales rep wants Tayler to try. Throughout the early afternoon, more will arrive, just in time for prep; most simply carry a box in their arms or hoisted up on their shoulder, some wheel a hand truck. After signing for the sea beans, Tayler brings a handful back to the table, extending an open palm to offer a taste to the team.

Thomas pops one in his mouth. "That tastes like going to the beach," he says, with a drawl that gives away his Mississippi childhood.

"And then," says Tayler, teeing up the meat course, "dry-aged strip loin, which we're getting from Slagel, and tomato that we're dehydrating just to intensify the flavor. We'll probably cut the tomato in half, sear it on the plancha so you get an even richer, caramelized flavor to it. A red wine, almost-broken-vinaigrette-type sauce with a little beef jus, and then we'll probably use some of the rendered fat, and then finish with French sorrel. And Chef mentioned maybe putting some of the carrots on there, so just be flexible on the carrots." She laughs about the poor itinerant carrots.

The qualifiers threaded throughout Tayler's instructions underscore the tentativeness inherent in this approach to weekly menu composition: "Maybe" stir a little lemon juice into the pesto to order, since doing it ahead of time will cause the nasturtium to brown; there "may" be additional herbs served with the mussels and shiso based on what's in the walk-in (ultimately, mint and basil made the cut); the braising liquid for the gem lettuce "might" be nothing more than oil and water so

Tomatoes dehydrate in the confines of an iCombi oven.

as not to compete with the high-impact vin jaune–butter sauce; the tomatoes on the beef dish will "probably" be cut in half; she "think[s]" the intermezzo will be garnished with tangerine lace; and "can't remember" what herb will be perched atop the peach tart.

The tomatoes for our dish are the first ingredient to which Tayler had turned her attention on arrival early Tuesday morning. As the team meets, about twenty tomatoes slowly dehydrate in the sauna-like confines of the Rational iCombi oven, the refrigerator-sized one in the corner of the open kitchen, so named for its ability to employ dry (convection) heat, moist (steam) heat, or a *combi*nation.

Lloyd Nichols, who started his sprawling business in a backyard garden

---

Just a few days prior, about sixty-five miles northwest of Chicago, amid rows of verdant foliage that extend to the horizon line, those tomatoes dangled from lush and overlapping vines in a field redolent of summer. From even a short remove, the greenery obscures one's view of individual crops, but the nose knows: Varieties of tomatoes, cucumbers, melons, peppers, carrots, and on and on and on and on flourish here. The field is one of several that comprise the more than six hundred acres owned or leased by Nichols Farm & Orchard, the business that, like Jack's fairy-tale beanstalk, sprang from a onetime hobby of Lloyd Nichols, starting in the 1970s.

In late April or perhaps early May, the petite seeds that grew into those comparatively huge Brandy-wines were sown in a tray of cells in one of the glass-walled greenhouses that dot the property on the original Nichols lot. Thereafter, the crew nurtured them on a steady diet of water fortified with a water-soluble mix of nitrogen, potassium, and phosphorus, with maybe trace elements of calcium nitrate, for three to four weeks. In late May, once any lingering threat of frost had receded, field workers gently transitioned the plants into the ground on one of the three hundred to three hundred fifty acres the family tills; the balance of the land is left for conservation. (Most of Nichols's tomatoes are field tomatoes, but some heirloom varieties are suited for hydroponic production from start to finish in the greenhouse.)

Once the tomatoes are in the ground, the focus shifts to protecting them from the elements and insects. Some plants are covered with one of the thousands of small, cylindrical metal cages in the nursery's agricultural armory. The cages are shaped like lampshade frames, onto and over which vines can be suspended to keep the fruit high and dry. Others are kept off the earth by twine suspended between stakes, and some are allowed to grow on the ground. In all cases, black plastic sheeting overlays the soil where stalks meet it. Under that plastic there snakes a drip irrigation system capable of watering ten acres at once, drawing from a nearby well. Depending on the weather, the farm will activate the system for up to eight-hour stretches.

In the summertime, when tomatoes are at peak ripeness, they are delivered to markets and restaurants the day after picking. That's the only quick part of the process. The tomato that co-stars in Wherewithall's strip loin dish requires a minimum maturation time of approximately seventy days; with other varieties it can be as long as ninety. All in, it's roughly three months from seed to plate, so the tomatoes eaten by guests of Wherewithall in our dish on July 24 are among the first that were seeded and planted in the spring.

Nichols plants up to *eighty* tomato varieties annually, but doesn't sell nearly that many. Call it a built-in insurance policy: With the acreage they farm and the volume of business they do, Nichols can absorb the loss of several failed varieties each season, with the best making it to market. This also enables Nichols to avoid employing an aggressive fungicide spraying program, thereby remaining true to their conservationist philosophy. And it allows them to shrug off maladies like bacterial wilt when they spy it on tomatoes in the field.

"That's the strategy I've always had," Lloyd says. "Let's plant as much as I can, and if I don't need it all, that's okay."

—

Lloyd Nichols, founder of this sprawling operation and the younger of two sons of working-class parents in Chicago proper, was born on August 6, 1945, the day the American military bombed Hiroshima, Japan. His father owned a small trucking concern; his mother functioned as his dad's assistant. In 1948, his father transitioned his business into the first air freight delivery service operating with C-46 cargo salvage planes out of Midway Airport, an industry that evolved over time into the likes of FedEx.

Lloyd Nichols was an average student, bored by academics but fascinated by gardening. His father gifted him a portion of the family's backyard garden, and young Lloyd planted radishes, peas, and other vegetables, and delighted in playing in the dirt. By the time he turned sixteen, cancer had claimed his mother, his older brother had enlisted in the service, and Lloyd lived alone with his father until he himself joined the Navy after high school; he was in boot camp when John F. Kennedy was assassinated in November 1963. He served until 1967, two of those years on the aircraft carrier *Enterprise,* a model of which today is docked on a bookshelf in his home at the Nichols compound. He was stationed in Japan while Vietnam escalated, and spent his last year of service in Kodiak, Alaska, at a Coast Guard airbase rescue-and-weather facility.

Following his service, Lloyd returned to Chicago and a wealth of employment opportunities. After a few fits and starts elsewhere, friends connected him with a job in ramp services for TWA at O'Hare Airport. Ramp service is "the guys who load the mail, air freight, baggage, cargo, put on the meals—I did all of those things," says Lloyd. He specialized in *commissary*, or stocking galleys with food and alcohol, at a time when airline meal service was luxurious.

In 1969, he bought a home in the suburb of Lombard, about twenty miles due west of the city. The house boasted a substantial yard where Lloyd fashioned a quarter-acre garden he packed with "everything you can eat." (Like cooks, farmers who aren't born into an agricultural family usually require a portal, and this was his.) In the summer, when the crops popped, neighbors gawked at the spectacle like daytime Christmas lights. In time, he bought a bigger house, on a half-acre lot, then purchased an adjoining half-acre when it became available, planted himself a bigger garden, and hooked up with Doreen Dowd, a fellow airport employee whom he went on to marry.

In the early 1970s, the couple moved to Wheaton, Illinois, where a chance drive past a farm with a sign outside reading GOATS FOR SALE sparked Lloyd's interest

Nichols field workers pick crops in the busy summer season.

in animal husbandry. Reflexively, as if they were convenience store impulse items, he purchased a few. At home, he hammered together a corral and a structure where they could shelter from the elements. In the pre-Internet, pre-YouTube days, Lloyd picked up the fundamentals of goat farming through a conversation with the farmer, supplemented with how-to books. "You don't have to have a PhD in animal husbandry to have a herd of goats," he says. In time they added a Jersey cow and some pigs.

Lloyd and I are interviewing outside his and Doreen's home at a glass-topped all-weather table, sipping iced tea in the August sun. At seventy-six, he maintains an action-figure physique. With his craggy visage, cargo pants, and Carhartt work shirt, he'd appear right at home on a battlefield, chomping a stogie and barking orders. That is, until he begins speaking and reveals himself to be a gentle, perpetually wonderstruck soul. On greeting me about an hour earlier, he ushered me into a golf cart to tour the property; within seconds, he'd pulled the vehicle over to yank a small wild plum, about the size of a ping-pong ball, off a tree. "Pop that one," he said, handing it to me.

I took a bite and was surprised by its peachy flavor. Lloyd grinned as he watched me, still enthusiastic after all these years.

Back to the mid-1970s, and those goats: He milked them a few times daily, and taught himself to make goat cheese, one of the "it" ingredients of the time. And, of course, the family reaped the benefits of the cow (milk) and pigs (bacon and pork).

When he learned that his deed covenant didn't allow for farm animals, it was a gut-check moment; though still just a hobby, he refused to give it up, and went looking for a home that was zoned for agriculture.

He and Doreen were taken with a model home in Lisle, and essentially had it recreated on a ten-acre ag lot in Marengo (where Nichols Farm & Orchard is based) in 1977. The Nicholses established an ambitious (for its time) four-acre garden where they grew asparagus and other vegetables. "Oh, everything," says Lloyd. In 1978, a friend suggested he could profit from his surplus by selling it at a farmers' market, back when securing a spot required nothing more than asking permission. (There were precious few Chicagoland farmers' markets at the time—one in Evanston and one in Oak Park, and both were eager for participants.) They loaded up Lloyd's pickup truck with whatever the Nicholses could spare, and the friend took it to market, where he pocketed a few hundred dollars. Lloyd saw an opportunity: He could pick the produce fresh on market days, sell it there himself, earn some extra cash. The following year, he signed up for markets in Evanston and Skokie and grew the garden from four to six acres. He and Doreen arranged their airport work schedules so they'd have weekends off. They'd prep on Friday, spraying produce clean with a garden hose and readying as much as possible for market.

This was in the ascendant days of Americans' food savvy—well into the Julia Child era and still at the nascency of New American restaurants. Nichols credits the enthusiasm and receptiveness of customers who were flowering into foodies, mostly faculty from Northwestern University in Evanston, for the eventual success of their business, and for his own adventurous spirit.

"I started doing things that other people didn't think about," he says. "I would pick my squash when they were little babies, and bring squash blossoms in. You had to be sophisticated back in the seventies to appreciate baby squash and little stuff." He folded heirloom tomatoes into the mix, and delicate little beans and little-known eggplant varieties, and the growing crowds lapped it up, eager to take food home and play around with it.

Lloyd's extrovert nature and enthusiasm proved contagious. "That's the key," he says. "If you don't enjoy something yourself, it's very hard to sell it to anybody. But if you go to a market, and you ate it yourself, and you thought, man, this is really tasty, boy, it's not hard to convince people, *This is worth eating, folks.*"

He pauses, then adds: "I don't know how many people I've educated into eating different vegetables in their life." Now in the winter of his career, Lloyd leaves the markets to others, but a version of this proselytizing by palate continues via certain employees of the farm, like Steve Freeman, whom I met on a visit to Green City Market with Tayler and Thomas. Steve was strolling the Nichols encampment and nonchalantly slicing slivers off a peach, wordlessly offering them to customers as they browsed.

For *thirteen* years, as the Nicholses added markets to their rounds, the couple also maintained their airline jobs. Lloyd worked the markets in the daytime, then bagged any unsold fruits and vegetables and headed to an afternoon or night shift at the airport, selling the leftovers to co-workers. Doreen helped on Saturdays and Sundays. Somewhere in there they raised three kids.

"My kids probably resent me because I spent so much time working," he says. "I didn't have time for Little League and those kind of things. But we did take vacations in the winter; we could shut down the place."

To focus on their rapidly expanding fruit and vegetable operation, Lloyd and Doreen jettisoned other parts of the farm, like animal husbandry.

About a year after purchasing the lot, secure in the farm's profitability and potential, they bought ten adjacent acres. Then in 1981, another ten acres on the other side, for a total of thirty. It was about that same time that Lloyd began networking with the regulars at a local gin mill, seeking workers to help pick and pack. One drinking buddy, a former machinist, connected him with some young Latinos who helped on an as-needed basis, mostly on Fridays and Saturdays. The operation developed in fits and starts: A wash rack was added at the barn, and by the mid-1980s, the farm had a few part-time employees. Doreen, meanwhile, stayed on in her airline job "until they retired her."

To this day, Lloyd doesn't consider himself a farmer. "To me, a farmer, essentially, is a commodity [farmer]," he says. "Guys doing corn, beans, wheat. Or animal husbandry with a dairy. I've always been what I considered a market gardener. I was growing vegetables for a market."

The farm's inroads into the restaurant industry developed more slowly, owing to a combination of early market hours (antithetical to a chef's working and waking schedule) and the prevailing attitude that they could get the same stuff from a wholesale market. But a few early adopters emerged: Paul Kahan, who also was Slagel's first chef customer, and Michael Ponzio, now of the Union League Club. To be competitive, Lloyd pored over seed catalogs and grew, or tried to, a little of everything, eventually nurturing hundreds of crops.

For such a successful business, it's remarkable that Nichols didn't grow out of a long-held dream, but rather incrementally, based on demand and opportunity, from a mere hobby. Today, Lloyd says that if his sons, Nick, Todd, and Chad, weren't interested in being a part of the business, he would have long since downsized.

In peak season, which we're in the midst of right now, tomatoes are picked by hand the day prior to delivery to a restaurant or a farmers' market. They're brought to Nichols's cleaning and packing facility on River Road, where they're rinsed by a team member at a washing station in the hangar-like structure and gathered in plastic bins to air-dry. The bins are then set in a cooler where they'll stay until the packing team arranges them in boxes bound for their destination.

The primary methods by which restaurants receive product from independent farms is directly via door-to-door delivery by the farmer themselves or a delivery driver the farm employs, or by visiting the farms' stands at local farmers' markets.

During the seasons that permit it, Tayler and/or Thomas visit the Green City Market—a sprawling Brigadoon of all things edible—in Mary Bartelme Park in the city's West Loop on Wednesdays and Saturdays. There they replenish their inventory, especially from farms that don't deliver to them, including Smits Farms, from which they purchase the thyme and rosemary for our dish. But most of the restaurant's proteins (fish, poultry, and meats) and produce are delivered directly to them by farms located within a roughly one-hundred-twenty-mile radius of Chicago. (Dry goods mostly arrive in mammoth trucks emblazoned with the logos of national gourmet suppliers like Chefs' Warehouse and Rare Tea Cellar.)

Marc Hoffmeister at the outset of his day, around three A.M.

For a sense of what deliveries entail, I meet Marc Hoffmeister at Nichols Farm's cleaning and packing facility at 3:30 A.M., electric light beaming in Spielbergian shafts from the structure's handful of loading docks. The sky above may be dark as squid ink, but here the business day is well underway: Clusters of workers in T-shirts and work pants swarm each dock, and if you're still shaking the sand out of your cranium as you navigate from one end of the hangar-like structure to the other, you run the risk of getting pancaked by a forklift. Everyone seems entirely too energized and enthused for this hour of the morning. Take, for instance, the man who speeds past me in a forklift.

"Mr. Fried-man!" he hollers. It's Steve Freeman, that Nichols team member I met at the Green City Market.

"Mr. *Free*-man!" I manage back, smiling through a yawn.

This being August, the perfume of peaches owns the air. Trucks bound for farmers' markets require a team to pack them; those being cargoed for restaurant deliveries are managed by lone specialists like Marc Hoffmeister, who's already there, at the backmost dock, organizing an array of boxes emblazoned with a generic FARM FRESH VEGETABLE logo, most with the name of their destination restaurant scribbled in black Sharpie in a corner of the fold-down top.

Marc is fit and spry, with a tight core and muscular legs that belie his sixty years, as does the enviable black of his hair and goatee. His khaki shorts, forest-green Nichols tee, and affability lend him the air of your favorite camp counselor. But don't be fooled. Yes, Marc is personable, and funny. But he also, to borrow a line from the *Taken* movies, possesses a very particular set of skills. He is, in fact, relative to most other drivers what a Navy SEAL is to a high school crossing guard.

He's also, alas, human, and subject to corporeal wear and tear. He's come to believe that back-support belts only serve to *weaken* one's spine and abdominal muscles, so doesn't use one, though a battered black lumbar support wedge rests on his driver's seat. He fends off muscle tweaks with a daily prework hot shower, stretching routine, deep-knee bends, coffee, and breakfast. He arrives loose, caffeinated, fueled up, and ready to go.

During the COVID pandemic, Nichols developed a CSA program, selling and delivering boxes weekly to homes or hub-locations from which orders are picked up by nearby customers. Boxes bound for those destinations bear small labels imprinted with individual customers' names, a reassuring glimmer of organization among a seemingly haphazard spray of boxes on the cement floor.

"I might look like I'm all over the place," Marc tells me, gesturing at the mess. "But there's a system."

And here's the first of Marc's powers: He performs most of his work without the aid of computerized gadgets save for his mobile phone—surprising and impressive in the digital age. Armed only with his eyes and a ballpoint pen, he crosschecks the boxes against a stack of invoices fastened to his clipboard, ensuring that his freight is complete. Then he piles boxes on his "two-wheeler" (that's *hand truck* to you and me), and loads them into his truck—a 2018 Chevrolet Express 4500 with a sixteen-foot box (shorthand for the sixteen-foot-long cargo area; this one is eight feet wide) and a Thermo King refrigeration unit (*reefer* for short). The day's last deliveries go in first, that is, at the back. Also at the back, on the passenger side, stands a metal utility rack on which Marc places flats of delicate greens and inverted box tops that he's repurposed as trays for cherry tomatoes.

Another employee—a wisp of a woman I'd put around sixty with graying blond hair and a hitch in her step—stops to politely ask me what I'm doing there. I tell her about the book project. She nods, smiles kindly, gestures around at the co-workers buzzing about: "All the people nobody sees."

This is still a transitional time in the COVID era so Marc and I have a chat about our mask policy for the day. "I'm Pfizered up," he offers, meaning vaccinated. I tell him that I am, too. We agree to keep the windows down and our masks in our pockets so they can be strapped on at stops along his route where it's required by management, or the staff wear them voluntarily.

By 4:40 A.M. Marc and I are on the road, fueling up at a gargantuan Road Ranger service station on US 20, near Hampshire. Then it's onto I-90 South, aka the Jane Addams Memorial Tollway, which becomes the Kennedy Expressway on the other side of O'Hare Airport. Hours into Marc's workday, the highway's a river of headlights though the sky retains its nocturnal blackness. We pull off in northwest Chicago and cruise into the desolate parking lot of an Eli's Cheesecake at 5:30 A.M. This is our first stop of the day: a

CSA pick-up location for farmers' market customers. Melons have recently come into season, adding heft to the boxes. Outside a set of glass doors, Marc stacks six boxes, plus one for Eli's cafe, containing melons, tomatillos, beets, and garlic.

Many of Marc's colleagues avail themselves of a routing app like Circuit Route Planner or RoadRUNNER Rides: You punch in all of your destinations, and it sequences them logically, *then* functions as a GPS, essentially reducing the driver to a human liaison between app and vehicle. Marc, a Chicago native, knows the city's nooks and crannies, traffic patterns and rhythms. *And he don't need no stinkin' GPS.*

"This is all stuff I learned when I was a kid," he says, imparting the organizing principles of Chicago's street plan: Madison Street is the "zero" point for north–south; State Street is "zero" for east–west, and so the center of the city's grid is the intersection of Madison and State and each block moving outward from there equates to 100 address numbers.

Marc's cultural breakdown is half Assyrian and half German, with a family tree whose roots extend to both the culinary industry and the city of Chicago: His maternal grandfather was a chef at the historic Palmer House Hotel in downtown's Loop area, and his father-in-law served as a sergeant with the 18th District on the city's Near North Side. Marc was born and raised on the Far

North Side, in East Rogers Park, just inland from Lake Michigan. After high school, he worked for an excavator, and in his twenties partnered with a friend in a remodeling and construction business. He's been a draft beer restaurant sales rep, and was a concrete laborer for the city until budget layoffs ended that after nine years. Next he moved to Crystal Lake, a midsized city about fifty miles northwest of Chicago, where he made his living as a salesman for a medical supply company, but was let go when they pared down their routes. That's when he set his sights on Nichols, which he knew from the Evanston farmers' market. He looked up the farm's address and headed there. Lloyd hired him on the spot.

A little past first light we ease up to a house on the northwest side of the city along what Marc calls an "alley"—a bank of row houses opposite corresponding storage garages across the street. There he leaves ten CSA boxes plus one for the host. That's the arrangement: Residents who volunteer their homes as pick-up locations receive a freebie for their trouble. (The drop-off locations double as pick-*up* locations for used boxes; yesterday Marc rounded up about one hundred.)

Except in extreme circumstances, Marc doesn't secure signatures or snap digital photographs of shipments resting safely on porches as proof of delivery the way, say, Amazon couriers do. "If people steal," he explains with what's quickly emerged as a characteristic fusion of wisdom and humor, "they're looking for a phone, not a box of beets."

Sunlight bursts upon skyscrapers as we continue on our way, and the city rouses around us. Slowly, we're synching up with the world, or it with us. Commuters wait at bus stops, joggers sweat through their kits in the mid-summer swelter.

Our first restaurant stop is Longman & Eagle, a modern iteration of a historic Chicago inn, complete with whiskey bar downstairs and rooms for rent on the second floor. Something on the invoice sets Marc's left eyebrow atwitter. His Luddite ways have screwed him—he's short one box of corn. There should be three for this restaurant, in addition to the squash and heirloom tomatoes packed into other boxes.

"There's always a monkey wrench," he says, shaking his head. You or I might panic at a missing box of corn, but Marc has seen and done it all before. He decides to loan himself a box from another order, with hopes of replenishing it by swinging by the Nichols tent at the Green City Market. (The other option would have been to short another customer one box and have it dropped off the next day.)

One of the cooks, dressed head to toe in black, is already in the kitchen and appears in the doorway.

"I haven't seen you in a while," says Marc, a natural and earnest kibitzer. "What time did you get here?"

"Five."

Back in the truck, the driver's seat morphs into a command center. Marc calls around to various colleagues, finally reaching Nick Nichols on the farm in Marengo, and asks him to let Steve Freeman, who's honchoing the farm's Green City Market encampment today, know he'll be swinging by to take a box from him.

"That's a good pivot when you can do it," he says, mic-dropping the clipboard into the black plastic chasm between driver and passenger seat.

Looking back later, the morning to this point will prove to have been both harbinger and microcosm of the hours ahead: Marc is personable and adaptable, and both qualities are essential to his work, the way a poker face and bullshit detector are to investigative federal agents. In the suburbs or country, parking and unloading a truck pose no challenge to mind or heart rate. Major American cities, on the other hand, present as veritable obstacle courses: traffic, a scarcity of available spaces that are scaled or zoned for trucks, and the threat of a parking enforcement officer lurking around every corner. (Practically speaking, parking tickets are a cost of doing business, but it's a point of pride not to incur one. Marc can't remember the last time he was ticketed, thanks in part to compassionate cops who accepted his claim that "I'm not parking. I'm making a delivery.")

En route to our next stop, Marc reveals to me that there's an overriding strategy to the day: The goal is to arrive at Brü, a hipster caffeine parlor on Milwaukee Avenue in Wicker Park, around eight or eight-thirty, a beat ahead of the worst morning traffic. This will in turn enable him to ride off into the sunrise, to Lincoln Park and then to suburbia, confident in the knowledge that he's equipped some of the best restaurants in Chicago with precious fruits and vegetables for . . . whatever it is they make in there. Marc and his wife, Jena (pronounced like "Gina"), are not really "out-to-eat people," as he puts it. They don't live in the city, she went vegetarian eight months ago, his work schedule isn't compatible with fine dining, and it's expensive.

A few quick stops later and as seven A.M. approaches, we're cruising east, in the general direction of Lake Michigan. We dock in front of Maple & Ash, a modern steakhouse and seafood restaurant, in a loading zone on Maple Street, around the corner from the delivery entrance.

Maple & Ash's cooks operate out of two kitchens, one on the third floor and one on the fourth. Accordingly, Marc splits the order and will make two trips; he stacks the two-wheeler up to its handlebars with boxes bearing corn, cherries, sweet-skinned cucumbers, and Tropea onions, and uses his fob to lock the truck. (He has a special affinity for this model because he can keep the reefer running even when the truck is locked.) We walk around the corner to a back alley, up to an un-marked door, and Marc shifts into secret-agent mode: He punches in a long code—five or six digits—from memory and we're in a shadowy employees-only corri-dor. A quick elevator ride to the third floor and we're in a clubby, wood-paneled restaurant space—closed and deserted at this hour—that conjures the Caribbean, prompting a sudden, unfashionably early craving for dark rum and contraband cigars.

"Morning, you guys!" Marc bellows as we roll into the kitchen, a narrow galley where a handful of cooks wearing pandemic-era surgical masks (we've put ours on) are already hard at work with the morning's prep—slicing vegetables, butchering fish and meat, sautéing that which can be sautéed in advance, cooled, and re-heated during service.

"I brought you a bunch of great stuff," Marc contin-ues, tipping the two-wheeler forward, then back, to ease the cargo off. "Great fruits and vegetables for you!"

The team smile and nod.

Even just unloading a delivery truck is physical work.

Back at the elevator, his mask lowered, leaning an elbow on the two-wheeler, Marc picks up with his intermittent running narration. "This elevator, when it's busy, there's another one around the corner," he says. As if I wouldn't believe him, he gestures me to the other elevator, flanked by two stanchions with a velvet rope suspended between them. "You remove the rope and—boop!—you're downstairs."

The elevator's taking a while to show up, so he shares a little more intel: "If you need a washroom," he says, indicating a door tucked into a recess along a nearby corridor, "that's a good one."

—

We head back outside and around the corner to load the two-wheeler up with deliveries for the fourth floor. In our short time indoors, the sun has climbed higher and vehicles of every shape, size, and color now clutter up the street.

Marc spots a paving truck near the alley that leads to the delivery entrance, and picks up his pace so he can get in and out before the truck backs around the corner onto Maple Street, where it might box him in. This isn't paranoia: "One time," he tells me, "a Sysco truck blocked the alley." A pause for dramatic effect, then a shrug: "They [the building's powers that be] let me in the front."

In *these* minutes, more truths have emerged: Big-city high-rises constitute universes unto themselves, with their own fiefdoms, elevator banks of varying efficiency, security protocols, amenities (if applicable), and workarounds. The morning gradually assumes a behind-enemy-lines tension as Chicagoans clog streets, fill elevators, and generally get in the way. Marc is on a mission, and superintendents, security guards, commuters, and traffic cops inadvertently conspire to thwart him. And so, every stop on his route is a problem to solve, a solution to be finagled, a test of his improvisational skills and the limits (if there are any) of his sprezzatura: where to stash the truck, which point of entry to each destination offers the least resistance, what to do if nobody's on hand to receive an order. (At some point in the day, maybe owing to sleep deprivation, I fantasize pitching a reality-show concept: *Delivery Wars!*)

Challenges are baked into some venues, and Marc recounts them with gusto. Like, for example, the day prior, Steve Freeman had to make *three* trips to the *sixty-seventh* floor of the Metropolitan Club. I've been helping Marc a little, loading the two-wheeler or carrying flats of delicate cherry tomatoes. And so, I can commiserate.

"Man," I say, shaking my head solemnly.

Turns out, that's nothing. As we breeze past the Art Institute of Chicago, Marc bemoans its impenetrability; he has yet to identify a lever to pull, a button to push, a loophole to exploit, a gatekeeper to flip, to make it more delivery-friendly—you *have* to park *three blocks* away. One time, to transport an ungodly amount of produce for a wedding, he had to do that and make *ten* trips to and from the truck. Trust him: You don't even want to know how much time *that* ate up.

"*Jesus*," I moan.

By seven-fifteen, we're cruising State Street, that grand, expansive, Frank Sinatra–lauded thoroughfare, its signature American magnificence arrayed before us, and minutes later we arrive in front of the Chicago Athletic Association, a nineteenth-century skyscraper that's been reinvented as a hotel with seven food and beverage options within its confines. It's a mammoth order: nine boxes bearing melons, French beans, green beans, heirloom tomatoes, cucumbers, Tropea onions, a full case of eggplant, and a flat of cherry tomatoes. We get off easy today, having to make only two trips with the two-wheeler.

A few more quick stops and suddenly we're trudging along a gloomy, otherworldly mashup of an alley, a tunnel, and a parking garage that, to my eye, extends endlessly ahead of us. Marc explains that we are on "Lower Michigan," an alternate thoroughfare that runs *under* Michigan Avenue for several blocks to the north and south of the Chicago River, and manifests as a double-decker bridge *across* the river. "This is like the bowels of the earth," he laughs over the truck's rumble. "You can take it from one end of downtown to another, but I got friends who won't ever come down here."

At 8:00 A.M., we pull up outside the Italian gourmet market Eataly, home to multiple restaurant concepts including a market osteria, a pizza and pasta concern, and a Lavazza caffè, as well as cooking classes. Today, Marc's delivering melons, Sungold tomatoes, and cucumbers to the osteria, and *forty* pounds of heirloom tomatoes to La Pizza & La Pasta.

At our next stop, we find ourselves underground again, this time beneath the Reid Murdoch Building, a landmarked redbrick structure with a clock tower at its center, that's home to the headquarters of Encyclopedia Britannica and also to River Roast, a modern American tavern-style restaurant. Suddenly, we're confronted with two pairs of loading docks separated by a narrow dead-end service lane. It's dark and grimy, and massive trucks jockey for position, gears grinding, wheels shrieking. Even Marc evinces a rare look of consternation. He harbors no love for these tight quarters and the potential for being boxed in by a colleague unmindful of the social contract. A truck that's idling in our path kindly backs up to enable Marc to back into his desired dock, replenishing his faith in his fellow drivers.

We carry four cases of corn and a flat of cherry tomatoes up a narrow, black steel stepway, corroded in places, and arrive at the delivery door to River Roast. Marc presses the service bell several times, but there's no answer. This never used to happen, he tells me, theorizing there's no one available to answer the bell due to the staffing shortage that's broken out during COVID.

He stacks the boxes on the landing, creates a makeshift platform by stacking a few milk crates that have been conveniently left there, then gingerly places the flats of cherry tomatoes on top—offering as much care and protection as he can as he leaves these delicate little tomatoes to the mercy of whatever may lurk down here.

"There's no other option," Marc says with a fatalistic shrug. He calls Nick Nichols to let him know the situation and head off any possible complaint from the restaurant.

After a few hours of observation, I'm in awe of Marc's capabilities. And so it makes me a little sad when he shares that some of his friends tell him he's doing grunt work.

"I like what I do," he insists. "I like the people I work with. I like the customers. It's fulfilling to me. It's a workout. I enjoy it."

We emerge into daylight and the stress gradually falls away. After a quick stop at avec River North, around 8:45 A.M., we head to a mystery stop, a new one on the route, about which Marc has been musing all morning. He's been calling it "Bain," evoking the unintelligible Tom Hardy villain in the third Christopher Nolan *Dark Knight* movie. When I see the name scribbled in Sharpie on the box, I learn it's actually *BIÂN* (pronounced bee-YAHN, an approximation of "beyond"). In the Small World Department, it's my friend Kevin Boehm's elegant, exclusive urban retreat, mingling elements of a health club, spa, medical center, and restaurant. The address is 600 West Chicago Avenue, which sounds straightforward, but this is virgin territory for Marc, so he hasn't yet decoded the best place to park, the best entrance, which doorman or security guard he can press into his service. Plus, occupying a corner location, its main entrance is unclear.

And so we turn onto North Larrabee Street where a doorman, making exaggerated throwing motions with his arms, directs us to a loading dock way down the road, away from West Chicago Avenue. We start that direction, but Marc quickly knows it can't be right, so he makes a turn hoping to get back to West Chicago Avenue, lodging instead in a cul-de-sac.

The quest for the proper entrance is taking entirely too long and we're hemorrhaging time, but Marc doesn't betray so much as a whiff of anxiety.

"Something I've learned," he says spinning the steering wheel to execute a three-point turn, "is, one way or another, it's gonna get off the truck. We don't come back [to the farm] with *anything*."

He finally locates the gold-framed doorway on West Chicago Avenue through which members pass into the great BIÂN. In front there's a drop-off/pick-up slip intended strictly for valet parking. This isn't conjecture; a sign eradicates any doubt. But Marc knows this is the best place to park because it's private property immune to the city's regulations, and so, unless the uniformed attendant decides to force the issue, there's no threat of a ticket. Assiduously avoiding eye contact, Marc loads up the two-wheeler, and marches into the building with an urgency that suggests he's a transplant medic delivering freshly harvested human organs. It works: The attendant clearly recognizes something isn't kosher, but declines to protest.

From here, it's downhill skiing: We drive the roughly two miles to Wicker Park and the promised land of Brü. We missed our self-imposed target arrival time, but only slightly, pulling up at 9:00 A.M. The street is blessedly free of parked cars and Marc stations the truck right out front. Brü's a pick-up spot for CSA boxes and Marc makes multiple trips with them on his two-wheeler, disappearing into Brü for minutes at a time—no doubt chatting up the baristas—then returning for the next load, delivering thirty in all.

We've been relieved of a massive literal and figurative weight. Five hours after pushing off from the Nichols warehouse, the truck is nearly empty. We treat ourselves to a coffee to celebrate, then head to Green City Market, where Marc bolts from the truck, returning in less than a minute with a box of corn to replenish the one he swapped in at Longman & Eagle.

At 10:00 A.M. we make a drop at Galit, a Middle Eastern restaurant on North Lincoln Avenue, mere steps from the alley where John Dillinger was shot and killed; periodically during the day, tour groups devoted to the city's criminal heritage pass by and guides detail the bank felon's demise through a megaphone. Inside, we meet chef Zach Engel, a young, bearded, and affable guy who gabs it up with Marc.

As big a city as Chicago is, its restaurant ecosystem is intimate: Zach buys copious amounts of za'atar from Smits, the same farm whose thyme and rosemary flavor our dish's red wine sauce, and is expecting Butternut Sustainable Farm's Jon Templin, who will also be dropping off a delivery at Wherewithall, shortly after Marc departs. *And* he just recently visited Slagel to cook a dinner as part of the farm's guest-chef series held in the event space on the edge of LouisJohn Slagel's property.

Our last stop is at 10:15 A.M., at Dear Margaret, where we visit with chef Ryan Brosseau. I leave Marc here. He'll head back out to Evanston for a few final drop-offs, and then back to Nichols.

Before we say goodbye, I ask this man of clear intelligence and off-the-charts social skills: Could he have been an office guy?

"Definitely not," Marc reflexively fires back. "It's not my makeup. I don't do well sitting still. I never really thought about doing that kind of work. I'm good with this."

And that is just one reason why many of the people encountered in these pages have gravitated to a life centered on restaurants. Sure, some have a passion for food, but just as many are metabolically incompatible with conventional professional careers. They want—*need*—to come as they are, be in perpetual motion, work with their hands, and have the freedom to chatter the day away. Until, that is, the time comes for them to pull off the seemingly impossible and, like a Chicago Bulls player circumventing the defense to make an eye-popping dunk, they are in their element, and their talent is plain for all to see.

Tayler wraps up the menu, shorthanding the desserts, since she'll be responsible for those: The intermezzo will be a spin on cottage cheese and fruit comprising Prairie Fruits Farm & Creamery's goat's cottage cheese, with celery gelatin and stewed cherries, and (probably) garnished with tangerine lace. The principal dessert will be roasted peach tart made with a semolina dough, almond frangipane filling, peaches, and an accompaniment of burnt sugar ice cream made with Okinawa black sugar,* then finished with raw young almonds.

---

* a Japanese sugar produced by boiling sugarcane juice over several hours, letting the resulting reduction cool into a black-brown solid, then crushing it into a powdery sweetener; it's more nuanced and deeply flavored than American brown sugar, which is made by adding molasses to white sugar.

The petits fours will be a nougat-like confection with pistachios and almonds. (After Tuesday night's service, when a different dessert has to be made on the fly for a walk-in party, the tart is changed to a roasted peaches, lemon custard, and chamomile composition.)

"You guys have any questions?" she asks.

Restaurants are teaching hospitals, and the dishes are the patients. The younger cooks are there to perform, but also to learn. And so nobody judges when Reuben asks if bronze fennel refers to a technique of cooking it, when it's actually an herb related to the bulbous plant, with purply fronds that taste faintly of licorice.

If this all sounds like a sadistic juggling act, it sort of is. The staff are locked in a love-hate relationship with Tuesdays. Johnny told me that in one team member's periodic review, they responded to the questions "What's the best thing about working here?" and "What's the worst thing about working here?" with the same answer: "Tuesday." The chefs' visions are carried out by cooks who didn't conceive the dishes themselves. Moreover, each dish conveyed in the menu meeting is something between a notion and a blueprint, subject to erasures and revisions, with a firm and fast-approaching deadline.

The meeting concluded, the team stand in unison, pocket their notepads, unfurl and tie on their aprons, and make for the kitchens.

As Reuben hurries to his prep station downstairs, he passes by David Lund, a former Parachute sous chef who's riding out the pandemic by working with Johnny and Beverly on the partnership they've forged with Goldbelly, the online retailer, in their case to sell and ship Parachute's famed Korean fried chicken, and Korean *bing* bread and condiments to food enthusiasts nationwide. (As for many restaurants, the relationship is a new one, undertaken during the pandemic to help offset lost revenue.) David does his work at Wherewithall, and has commandeered the private dining room across the courtyard out back as a staging area for the boxes until UPS picks them up.

"Hey, Reuben, what's your day look like?" asks David.

"Prepping a new menu."

"Oh, so no idea yet."

They both laugh. I get the feeling this is a weekly bit, engaged in every Tuesday right after the menu meeting.

In any event, it's a long, pressurized journey into the week's first service as the individual dishes and over-all menu will be workshopped—the cooks executing first-drafts of the dishes, Tayler and/or Johnny sharing feedback and direction for course-correction—right up until the first snacks leave the pass.

3

Prep

Saturday night service continues at Wherewithall, the kitchen now pumping out a variety of courses in steady rhythm, and the dining room team shuttling them to their destination tables. On the sound system, Yo La Tengo's "Periodically Double or Triple" casts a retro, Sunset Strip vibe over the scene.

Johnny, having been home to spend time with the kids, has returned to the restaurant and visits with Tayler at the pass, jumping in as necessary to expedite, as when, around eight forty-five P.M., he dispatches Nooshâ to deliver the oats "risotto" to Table 12, who are now two courses away from being served our dish. (That Johnny won't don chef's whites or an apron at any point this evening is testament to how thoroughly he's shed old-school rigidity over the years.)

Johnny and Beverly are constantly struggling to find the right childcare for their nonconventional schedule. They often employ two nannies—one during the day and one in the evening. Currently, they're down a night person, but Beverly has arranged a sitter and plans to return later during this busiest service in more than a year.

The kitchen is a hive of nonstop activity tonight. Yet for all that's happening before our eyes, much of the work has been done in advance, during the prep day. In most restaurants, prep is repetitive: The same cooks do the same tasks daily. Some kitchens employ dedicated prep cooks who never see action on the line. Wherewithall operates on a common fine-dining model, fashioned after a traditional European structure, in which cooks prepare what can be made ahead of time for their own respective stations. But regardless of who carries out which task, this is what goes on by day in any restaurant—from a twenty-four-hour diner, where there's always some prep underway, to Chicago's Michelin three-star-rated Alinea, where it's done by day as at Wherewithall.

For the most part, mornings and afternoons are quiet here. Unless Jessica or Tayler are conducting an interview with a prospective employee in the dining room, or a meeting is taking place, the team is mostly focused on cooking. There's no music, as in some other kitchens. Downstairs, the only sounds are the hum of the beverage cooler and freezer, knives clacking on cutting boards, the tape on boxes being cut. Everybody moves with urgency, which is why—during prep and service—anyone approaching the stairwell that leads from the dish pit to the upstairs kitchen announces "Corner!" just before passing through the doorway to avoid colliding with a colleague moving in the opposite direction.

A smart and/or experienced cook will arrange their time according to what takes the longest. In the prep kitchen upstairs, Jenna starts by making the broth: In a huge pot, she slowly, over several *hours*, caramelizes twelve quarts of sliced onions. To this will be added sherry, leftover chicken stock from the walk-in, and beef bones and scrap that she'll have slowly roasted as the onions cooked. Just before service, she'll clarify the stock, season it with salt, strain it, and pour as much as possible into that tea kettle at her station, refilling it as necessary. (After Tuesday, she may start the broth at the end of the service and let it simmer overnight to save time the next day.) When it comes time for Thomas to butcher the strip loin, he'll do so in the open kitchen, in the same position he'll spend service; throughout the day and right up until straining-time, Jenna will toss whatever beef scrap that butchery may yield into the stock pot to intensify the broth's beefiness.

Once the broth is working, Jenna moves on to less time-consuming items on her punch list: She steams mussels open in olive oil, with citrus zest, shallot, and Thai chile, then picks the mussels and refrigerates them in their liquor until service. She also juliennes raw kohlrabi, wraps, and refrigerates it, and cleans, dries, wraps, and refrigerates mint and basil leaves. She thinly slices bread the restaurant purchases from Middle Brow, a local brewery and bakery, arranges the slices on a baking tray, drizzles them with olive oil, seasons them with salt, and bakes them until they are browned and crispy—these are the croutons for the optional cheese course. And she toasts pecans for cheese plates, finishing them with olive oil and salt.

Downstairs, the main prep area is a rectangular room framed by stainless-steel worktables. At the far end, with his back to the room, Thomas executes some of his tasks, which include elements of family (staff) meal. To his left stands Reuben, at a table along the perpendicular wall. Since they will tandem-cook and plate the main body of the meal—the appetizer, fish, and meat courses—during service, they divvy up the prep. Reuben is charged with, among other tasks, shucking and slicing baby corn, curing egg yolks, picking bronze fennel, trimming little heads of gem lettuce, and preparing the sauces, including the vin jaune sauce for the fish course and the red wine sauce for our dish, the meat course, which requires two pots: In one, Tropea onion, garlic, rosemary, bay leaf, and thyme are browned together in butter. In a separate pot the same five ingredients are heated in a bath of Wyncroft Shou (a blend of Cabernet Sauvignon, Cabernet Franc, and Merlot from the Michigan winery) and set to simmer and reduce almost to a syrup, then strained, the solids trashed. Come service, Reuben will warm the fat (butter) and Wyncroft liquid together in batches, whisking to blend them. On this Tuesday, this proved one of those blessed ideas that aligned with the chefs' vision on the first attempt, requiring scant course correction; on Wednesday, the second day of service, only minor adjustments were made to its preparation, like increasing the quantity of each aromatic to amplify their flavors.

Ironically, Reuben Tomlins—the Wherewithall team member least fond of Tuesday—was first attracted to cooking through culinary improvisation. As a child in Southern California, Reuben found gardens fascinating, and also enjoyed experimenting with his mother in the kitchen. His first happy memory of cooking occurred when he was eight or nine years old.

"She would give me free rein," says Reuben, standing at his prep table in the restaurant basement, his hands—apparently imbued with brains of their own—

shucking baby corn and shaving the little ears into coins on a plastic Japanese mandoline. "There was no recipe. I'd throw all sorts of weird things into a mixture and then we'd bake it and see how it turned out. It wasn't necessarily anything we were going to eat. It was completely weird: 'Oh, let's throw in cinnamon.' We'll throw in maybe some flour. We'll throw in some peanut butter. We'll throw in some peas from the freezer. We would just throw it in the oven and see what happened."

Baking is the culinary medium least suited to winging it; unlike much savory cooking, it almost always depends on exact quantities and weights, temperatures, and cooking times. So of course most of Reuben's childhood projects failed. But he and his mother sometimes found gold in their pan, like the dense, muffin-like concoction Reuben christened *transmogrifiers*, after a trippy device in the *Calvin and Hobbes* comics—a cardboard box with a dial fixed to its side that transformed the user into anything they desired. Reuben and his mother topped it with jam and proclaimed it a triumph. Tragically, because notetaking wasn't a practice in the Tomlins home, they never succeeded in recreating it.

Reuben found those exercises emboldening, which was no accident: His mother taught according to the Reggio Emilia method, which prioritizes the individ-

Reuben Tomlins in the midst of service

uality of each child and their ability to self-direct, and supports their exploration and expression through any number of "languages," including myriad art forms and crafts.

"They empower the kids," says Reuben. "They let the kids kind of dictate what they want to do, and they ask them questions about stuff rather than just putting words in their mouths. So she's always been very, '*You want to try something?* Try it. *How do you want to do it?* Did you think it would turn out this way?'"

Reuben was the only child born to his mother and father, a Tinseltown grip (the crew member on a film or television production responsible for lighting and related equipment). His parents partook of the Golden State's abundant culinary riches. They weren't restaurant groupies, but Reuben and his mother frequented farmers' markets, and both parents cooked—usually his mother because of her more regular working hours, though his dad enjoyed taking a shift when he was between gigs. Reuben's father was Irish and Italian from upstate New York; his mother of Eastern European Jewish background from Detroit. But there were no shepherd's pie, borscht, or kugel served at the family's dining table, where the only culinary nod to genealogy was pasta.

Reuben was an extroverted kid and natural athlete who skateboarded, surfed, and played soccer. He fantasized about becoming a television sports commentator but didn't pursue it. Neither did he go to college. His parents had saved for tuition, but by the time Reuben graduated high school, he was burned out on academics and—without a clear sense of direction—opposed squandering their money on something so amorphous.

Biding his time, he moved to central California and bunked with a buddy who was attending California Polytechnic State University, San Luis Obispo. Reuben took a job in the university's dining hall kitchen—*his* portal. The cooking was mostly rudimentary, if not robotic, like steaming precut vegetables dumped out of freezer bags. Even scratch cooking, like the preparation of pasta dishes, was performed on an industrial scale, in monstrous kettles, eliminating any possibility of nuance or finesse. Culinarily, the enterprise bore little resemblance to what goes on at a restaurant like Wherewithall, but Reuben "fell in love with the team aspect of it. Coming from a sports background, it all made sense: the camaraderie, *having* a team, working hard at something. It all just kind of clicked."

He doesn't consider himself a natural cook. Looking back he judges himself as downright awful in those salad days. But he worked hard and expressed an eagerness to learn, willingness to be molded, and excitement at the possibility of getting better and of maybe having found his calling. The dining hall's chef sensed this and invested time and attention in him. When she migrated to a position with on-campus catering, she brought Reuben with her. In the new job, he helped prepare food for university presidential functions or the president's modest suite at the football stadium, and special events. This marked an upgrade to more refined cooking, including finger food and composed dishes.

During this time, Reuben fell into a romance with a fellow Southern California native, Shelby. Around 2015, they moved to Portland, Oregon, which they'd both grown fond of on an extended road trip. In search of experience in a proper restaurant kitchen, he answered an ad and took a job down the street from their home, at a place that he remembers as an awful "Olive Garden-y" local chain restaurant. Even worse, the job posting was a bait-and-switch: He was hired to be a cook, but the restaurant was down a dishwasher, so that's what he did. Taking a glass-half-full approach paid off: When he was promoted to line cook after three months, he had already established a rapport with his co-workers.

The restaurant operated with kitchen managers rather than chefs. Dishes were set by the company; individual locations merely executed. They did high volume and he notched the essential first line cook experience he sought, but the location where Reuben worked was the smallest in the company—a sort-of farm league for the larger outposts. If a manager proved themselves there, they were promoted to the majors; if they couldn't hack it on such a small scale, they were cut loose. Reuben's location went through six managers in about a year, which he says made life there "miserable."

Despite all of that, this was the time when Reuben began to morph into a member of what we might call *the expressive food community*. *Oversimplification Warning*: The workforce in restaurants can be divided into two populations: those for whom it is a job, and those for whom it is a pursuit. Neither is inherently better than the other, but those for whom it's a pursuit don't leave the kitchen behind when they clock out. Instead, they devour cookbooks and chef-focused documentaries and streaming series for inspiration and guidance; keep tabs on the national and global restaurant scene on websites and social media; blow a huge percentage of their take-home pay on inspirational meals; and aspire to helm their own restaurants. Those getting closer to attaining chef status themselves might stage pop-ups to test-drive their developing style and repertoire. Reuben did all of that, save for the pop-ups, while marinating in Portland's burgeoning dining scene, eventually leaving his job for Pok Pok Noi, the second iteration of chef Andy Ricker's popular Thai restaurant, where a greatest-hits menu of his dishes was served. Reuben went deep, staying almost three years and working his way through every station: In a little hut outfitted with two Big Green Eggs and small-box charcoal grills, he grilled and smoked meats and vegetables, and worked the pok pok station, imported by Ricker from Thailand, that's essentially a three- or four-hundred-pound mortar and pestle. (The name *pok pok* derives from the sound of a wooden pestle scraping against a clay mortar.) Beyond amassing a valuable battery of techniques, Reuben developed his intuition for flavor considerations, such as *balance*. "Everything had a base of some sort of acid, some sort of salt, and then a spice," he remembers. "That's when I really started to examine that."

Then it was off to another local restaurant, Oven and Shaker, a wood-fired-oven eatery powered by Portland icon chef Cathy Whims in partnership with spirits professional Ryan Magarian. It would prove a brief stop on Reuben's way to another wood-fired spot, Tastebud, in Multnomah Village on the outskirts of the city proper, his first sous chef job. The owner, Mark Doxtader, originally had been a farmer who began rolling into farmers' markets with a trailer onto which he'd built a wood-fired oven, which in turn led to a pizza-focused restaurant that also offered a smattering of plated dishes.

"Everything was based on just using stuff from the market, stuff from local farmers," says Reuben. "Basically, everything we could get our hands on except for maybe just staples that you would get from other local purveyors. The menu always changed. Really, really fun stuff. That was the first experience I had with that, and that sort of blew my mind."

Suddenly, it all made sense: The childhood attraction to gardens, the extemporaneous cooking with his mother, the deepened interest brought on by his first kitchen jobs, and now the mingling of those predilections and passions. "I'd always gardened myself, or had vegetable gardens, and loved the thought of, *It would be really fun to have a place that just was farm to table*," says Reuben. "But I never had worked anywhere like that. And that changed everything for me."

Doxtader's extemporaneous process matched well with this young man who'd grown up improvising in the kitchen, though he learned the limits of his tolerance for spontaneity in this job. Initially, the sight of cooks scattering sliced peaches or pitted cherries over pizzas woke up the pessimist in him—even the daredevil who made the *transmogrifier* had to wonder, "How will that ever work?" But he found the resulting pies, with the fruit and molten cheese as inseparable as a sundae's ice cream and syrup, "amazing and beautiful." The restaurant also acquainted this lifelong gardening aficionado with heretofore unfamiliar ingredients, like cardoons, a slightly bitter kin of artichokes.

The true revelation, though, was working with wood-burning ovens, one of professional cookery's femmes fatales, capable of driving chefs mad as they attempt to understand and control her.

"That was something that really, really fascinated me and was really fun," says Reuben. "Every day, what you're cooking with is different. It's *alive*. It changes. The fire's not always the same; you don't just turn it to six and it's going to be on six. I don't think I ever mastered it, but *trying* to master it. . . . At times, you hate it when you're just trying to get dinner out, but I would say 90 percent of the time I absolutely loved it."

A year and a half later, the chef was fired and Reuben received a battlefield promotion from sous chef to chef. The adherence to seasonality and availability of ingredients made the transition challenging in some respects but ultimately also made it easier. Reuben stayed in the position for almost a year.

In 2019, Shelby was accepted to University of Illinois Chicago for graduate school in occupational therapy, and she and Reuben moved to Chicago, securing an apartment in Humboldt Park, on the border of Ukrainian Village. He'd felt qualified for the limited technical requirements of running Tastebud's kitchen, but didn't believe he was ready for full-fledged chefdom outside a wood-fired situation. And so he touched down in Chicago seeking a position on the line in a chef-driven restaurant with a more traditional menu. "You know, where there's really, really high standards to the plating, to the food, everything that goes into it," he says.

He was intrigued by several local possibilities, and planned to *stage* at many of them, until he began reading and learning about Parachute, and then trailed there.

"I was, like, *This is where I want to be*," he says.

He worked two stations before the pandemic descended and eventually, like so much of the current crew, migrated to Wherewithall.

Reuben thinks he will likely return to wood-fired cooking someday. Many cooks, especially those with aspirations of becoming chefs, keep a physical or digital notebook with lists and sketches of ideas for combinations, sauces, accompaniments, and full-fledged dishes. Often the notebooks also include recipes for vinaigrettes, stocks, sauces, and whatnot from prior jobs. Reuben only keeps a notebook for the latter, *not* as an ongoing dream file of dishes he plans to hone and enshrine on the inaugural menu if and when he hangs out his own shingle. For this cook, it's all about the moment.

"Right now," he says, "it's just learning techniques, having fun."

Each time Reuben produces a batch of sauce during service, he adds the requisite amounts of the aromatic-infused butter and red wine reduction to a saucepan. He brings it quickly to a simmer, whisking the whole time to integrate the flavors. The bubbling sauce that comes together derives its primary flavors from the produce and product of two independent farms owned and overseen by two very different men, both of whom—by a cosmic coincidence—were once bound for the pulpit . . .

Every morning at dawn, James Lester—proprietor and vintner of Wyncroft, situated about two hours from Chicago, around the east side of Lake Michigan—floors the pedal of his pickup truck, racing across the ninety-four-acre estate, leaning on the horn and blasting a shotgun into the air. He's not charging headlong into battle, nor has he gone stark, raving mad. The ritual is his deceptively humane way of training the wild turkeys and raccoons who populate the woods on the outskirts of his property to stay among the trees and clear of the grapes that will, in time, become the wines he makes, bottles, and sells. At dusk, he'll repeat the exercise. If, over time, any raccoons fail to get the message, he'll trap and relocate them to another forest nearby.

James doesn't look the sort to drive a pickup or brandish—let alone discharge—a shotgun. His Norseman's gray mane and beard suggest a man out of time, and his immediate surroundings do nothing to dispel that notion. Leave behind the contemporary two-story house with expansive glass windows that he shares with wife, Daun, the modest winemaking facility and tasting room across the driveway, and the cars parked there, and the modern world recedes.

The feng shui here is off the charts: An impeccably manicured grassy incline extends away from the residential and commercial section of the property, opening onto acres of neatly aligned rows of trellises on which small clusters of grapes are evenly spaced and immaculately maintained. The natural light here captivates. By day, it casts storybook beams across the grass. At night, as the sun sets, shadows stretch from the trellises across the lawn until darkness falls.

Love among the vines: James Lester and Daun Page.
©Miriam Teft 2023

Wyncroft ostensibly exists to grow grapes and produce and sell wine. It's also a manifestation of James's
long-considered and anecdotally tested beliefs about
conservationism, nutrition, and—yes—winemaking.

A child of the sixties and seventies, James came
of age in Bellevue, Washington, where his parents
enforced the strictures of the Seventh-day Adventist
Church, prohibiting James and his three sisters from
smoking cigarettes or drinking alcohol, and also from
dancing to—or even listening to—rock and roll. "It
was church music, or no music," he says.

The Lesters expected their children to express themselves clearly, with proper grammar (James's mother taught English), and do household chores. An outdoorsman by nature, young James requested garden and landscaping tasks and his mother accommodated, imparting her own passion and knowledge to him starting when he was seven. She taught him about plants, seeds, and pollination; he was so enamored by rhododendrons and azaleas that in his teenage years, he engineered a few hybrids.

"I enjoy being around plants," he says as we walk the winery property. "They don't talk back, they're not mean to you, and they respond very well to our attention. It's a very rewarding life-form."

James set out to be a church minister, a path that in retrospect was ill fated. He shared many of his contemporaries' suspicions and disenchantments, especially toward authority figures and institutions. When he moved to Michigan to pursue a master of divinity degree at Andrews University, he asked his instructors questions he dare not have posed at home. The response was inevitably a variation on "Well, such and such is so, and just don't question it"—which, in the parlance of the times, turned him off.

"That runs against my nature," says James. "I have a disdain and dislike of people who want me to believe something because they say so. I can think for myself.

I realized very quickly that I wasn't going to be a theologian."

Relieved of the family prohibition, he developed a quick and deepening respect for wine, especially French-style wines, that, given his predilections, naturally led to teaching himself the crafts of grape growing and winemaking. In that pursuit, he may not be a theologian by the dictionary definition, but he's as much philosopher-farmer as gentleman-farmer. Accordingly, his tour of Wyncroft begins not with a wine spiel, but with a primer on what he considers a greater mission: "We're very proud that we have a very diverse ecosystem on the farm."

For a convenient contrast, he casts a hand across the horizon line, indicating a neighboring farm that exclusively raises corn and soybeans. The trick? They plant genetically engineered Roundup-ready seeds that are resistant to the ubiquitous herbicide.

"Roundup chelates* all the minerals in the soil, including metals like magnesium and iron that plants need as micronutrients," James explains. "So he has to put artificial fertilizer on it." This yields abundant quantities of corn and soybeans, but renders the land otherwise unsuitable for growing or grazing. In his

---

* Chelation deprives plant pathogens of nutrients by minimizing their presence in the soil.

Grapes await pressing in the Wyncroft production room.
©James Lester 2023

far-from-singular view, the soil at that sort of farm essentially functions as a neutral medium for the roots, which must siphon nutrients not from the soil, but from fertilizer. For James, the Wyncroft property is a response and a rebuke to such unsustainable and depressing practices.

"We can't expect to keep doing this forever," he says. "Eventually human beings will disappear off the planet. Soil will be gradually replenished and the microbiome will once again go back into that soil, but it's going to take a while."

In the meantime, he explains, we humans can't derive proper nutrition from foods nourished by the agricultural equivalent of a feeding tube. "We're going to harm our bodies," he says. "Of course, a lot of big corporations are making billions of dollars selling genetically engineered seeds, fertilizers, Roundup. Giant diesel-guzzling monster tractors they use to plow things up. It's interesting that when human beings decide to raise something they destroy the habitats of literally thousands of organisms, from bacteria in soil to worms to insect population to all of the food chain being disrupted."

If you're wondering how all of this relates to Wyncroft's Shou, the classic Bordeaux blend of three red wine varietals (Cabernet Sauvignon, Cabernet Franc, and Merlot) that is the foundation of our dish's sauce, the answer is simple: Growing grapes with as much flavor and character as possible is the result of many of the same ideologies that drive the vineyard's practices.

"It turns out the things you do to make better grapes is best for the vine, too," he says.

All three varietals are fashioned from small grapes with—crucially—thick skins. To help foster that thickness, James applies tough love.

"I don't pamper my plants," he says. "We've all bumped into pampered human beings. They're usually spoiled, had everything handed to them, never had to work for anything. They treat other people badly, and seldom produce any virtue. In the case of a grapevine that has to struggle and find its own nutrients, it's the [converse] idea."

And so James doesn't water or fertilize the vines. At all. Nor does he employ Roundup or weed sprays on the ground beneath the trellises. Paramount to such practices is maintaining generous airspace all around the vines so they have easy access to both life-giving sunshine and cooling breezes. Even heavy rainfalls are quickly drunk up by soil, with gusto, and the grapes are gently, naturally dried by sun and wind. (To further stoke this dynamic, the vines face east, so are bathed in sunlight all day, from all sides.) James limits the number of clusters on each vine, spacing the clusters three feet apart—the large, *naturally* nutrient-rich root system beneath the soil therefore sustains a limited number of grapes. In addition to growing fruit of the desired size, thick skin, and flavor, good nutrition helps the vines survive the winter and be ready for the next year's growing season.

Like other farmers whose produce is present in our dish, James functions largely on intuition, which for him is aptitude's B-side. "A lot of aptitude is interest," he says. "If you're interested in something you're likely to have an aptitude for it. I also think there's natural love of something. When you love something, you put a lot of attention and *intention* into it." James spends time communing with the vines daily and has trained himself to spot visual cues of nutrient deficiency, usually a lack of boron or magnesium; for example, yellowing leaves indicate depleted magnesium levels, which he corrects with a mist of Epsom salts.

"The salts will be absorbed through the leaves, and within a week the vine is much greener," he says. "Like you might take vitamin C if you have a sore throat."

Another practice driven by instinct: When James, Daun, or one of the two farm workers they employ pull leaves off clusters or clip unnecessary canes, rather than cart them away, they scatter them in the rows between the trellises, then run a special mower over them to chop them up and ease their return to the earth. This isn't standard winemaking protocol, but a self-styled adaptation of one of James's childhood chores. Periodically, young James transferred the organic kitchen detritus his mother gathered in a small bin to a compost heap in the yard, then tended the heap with a garden fork, marveling at its gradual transformation into rich, black soil with plump earthworms happily feeding on its nutrients. If a plant on his family's property was ailing, James would pack some of that precious soil around it, then watch it heal in mere days.

"It's like a combination lock," he says of grape growing and winemaking. "It has to be coming from happy vines that are grown in the right kind of soil, with the right nutrients to create those flavors. It has to be made by a conscientious grower who's growing the grape himself or herself and so is intimately in touch with the rhythms of nature in the vine, knows exactly when to harvest that vine, is in charge of how many clusters are on each vine, is in charge of the health of the vineyard and the health of the soil, so that all those things can converge to make a great glass of wine."

"It's not unlike the concept of your book," he says, "where all these different things come together in this one dish. All *these* things come together in one glass."

Each year's growing cycle culminates in the harvest, a cherished time in any vineyard's calendar. In Michigan, Pinot Noir reaches maturity first, by late September. Cabernet Sauvignon matures in late October when those grapes ripen and turn from green to pink and finally to a deep purplish red—the change in color is referred to as veraison. Around the same time, Cabernet Franc grapes undergo the same transformation. (When only some varieties have changed color, it looks for a time like Christmas came early with the juxtaposition of red and green up and down the vineyard.) James also tastes along the way to gauge the optimal moment to harvest each grape: "As fruit ripens, acid descends and sugar ascends," he says. "When sugars

Edilberto (Eddy) Cassaruvias Avila, left, with James Lester
©Daun Page 2023

build up, and the acid is coming down, *and* flavor is coming up—*that*'s the sweet spot. It should have a big pop and give your salivary glands a squeeze."

As each varietal is ready, James, Daun, and their team, joined by a few volunteers, take to the trellises with surgical-grade stainless-steel clippers, taking down a row in about half an hour. The grapes are gathered in twenty-five-pound plastic lugs and transported to the onsite facility for pressing, aging, and—in some cases—blending.

—

James and Daun tend to the six acres of vines by hand with the help of two full-time workers, a father-and-son duo from Mexico. The father, Edilberto (Eddy) Cassaruvias Avila, is a native of the town of Pochutla in the state of Guerrero, born there in 1960. His family maintained a small cattle ranch on which they raised chickens, goats, and cows, and farmed beans and corn, mainly to sell to neighbors. He began working on the family farm at age six, planting crops and washing cattle. Education was a secondary consideration.

When his father died, the family dispersed. Edilberto worked construction and in factories, but desired a better quality of life for his wife and two children. In the mid-1980s, when he was about twenty-five, he came to the United States.

His American adventure began in New York City, where he roomed with five others in a small unit in a massive apartment building in the Bronx. He took a job downtown, washing dishes in a restaurant, and commuted on graffiti-covered subways. After a few years, at an uncle's behest, he took a job in a Japanese restaurant in Trenton, New Jersey.

Edilberto had swallowed the Hollywood version of the American dream whole, so the rigors of an immigrant life stunned him.

"You think the United States is going to be easy, like in the movies, you just get the money," he says.

"When I came here, we couldn't do anything because the jobs slowed down. I stayed in the apartment for two or three months, with no work." Fortunately, his roommates supported him through this time.

Traveling back and forth from Mexico to the United States in those days was easy, even as an undocumented worker, he says. North of the border, however, fear of the immigration authorities was constant. Raids, usually triggered by a tip from an anonymous caller, occurred regularly, and fellow immigrants disappeared in a flash, presumably deported, their possessions left behind. Consequently, Edilberto—a homebody by nature—rarely ventured out to bars or socialized outside his apartment building.

After four or five years and a brief return to Mexico, during which he fathered another child, he followed a cousin to Michigan, where he'd found work on a farm in South Haven. Edilberto lived in the cousin's camper. After enduring his first bitter midwestern winter there, he decided to seek a better situation, taking a job with the prior owners of the Wyncroft estate, and renting a small house from them on the edge of the property.

Today, Edilberto's responsibilities include tending to the vineyard, pulling grapes, landscaping, and maintaining the pressing and bottling facility and tasting room. It's strenuous and tiring, as it would be for anybody. But he's been lucky. Other than some soreness in

his knees that he knocks out with an occasional corti-
sone shot, he's been spared significant injury or pain.
Moreover, he *enjoys* working outside, which takes him
back to his childhood and keeps him fit and limber.

It's rare for an author to be able to interview an
immigrant farm worker in the United States with the
blessing of their employer, because so many farm workers in this country are undocumented. Even broaching
the possibility is something of a third rail. When James
mentioned in our interview that the vineyard has two
employees, Daun—who'd been sitting silently alongside
us outside the tasting room—jumped in to add, rather
pointedly: "*Documented*." Seizing on this I was able to
arrange an interview with Edilberto and a separate conversation with his adult son, Humberto Casarrubias.

In the early aughts, Edilberto consulted an immigration lawyer about obtaining a permit. The lawyer
advised him to marry an American woman or enlist a
sponsor who would write letters in support of his application. The owners of a nursery where he also worked
stepped up, writing those letters, and secured him a
permit, then a green card, for which he considers himself lucky; very few people he knows with similar
histories have managed to achieve documentation.
(His son is among them.)

Even with green card in hand, he found the 2016
presidential campaign season "a little scary," because

Smits Farms

of candidate, then president, Trump's anti-Mexican rhetoric, but never personally encountered any antipathy. "Everybody I know is very nice," he says.

The thyme and rosemary, the other principal components of our dish's sauce, hail from Smits Farms, a roadside operation in Chicago Heights, Illinois. (Smits also owns and operates farms in Steger and Beecher.) At the edge of the property, there's a dirt parking lot and a farmstand, and a stenciled sign promoting key crops and flowers in tall red letters. There's a compound of greenhouses closest to the road, and rows of herbs, forty types in all, that extend back six hundred fifty-eight feet to the property line. To the naked eye, the herbs are largely indistinguishable, green growths poking up through black plastic.

Chicago Heights is a small city about thirty miles south of Chicago, tucked into the corner formed by Lake Michigan and the Indiana state line, so close that the steeple of St. Joseph Church, in Dyer, Indiana, is visible from the farm. It's an apt metaphor for the business's genesis because—like James Lester—Carl Smits was once bound for the pulpit. A son of Lansing, Michigan, he attended Calvin University in Grand Rapids, with the intention of becoming a minister or pastor but a course in soil science, taken during his junior year to fulfill an elective requirement, spun him in another direction.

"It was one of my best classes ever," he says. "They stress that if you're going to farm, you have to build up your soil. For years, farmers have been taking from the soil but never really putting anything back. If you really want healthy soil, you have to put back."

The course aligned with a natural inclination toward the outdoors and a fondness for getting his hands dirty. As graduation came into view, he pondered the shape he wanted his career to take. He considered the possibility of missionary work, bringing the Gospel to people in another country, perhaps Guatemala, which he'd visited for a week during high school and loved. In preparation for such a path, he'd declared Spanish as a major. He also knew for certain what he *didn't* want: to be a church pastor in the United States, confined mainly to the indoors. His direction seemed clear, but at a jobs fair for pastors and missionaries, not one person had anything to offer in the way of a posting that would allow him to honor his love of God, Spanish, the outdoors, and soil science, ideally in a foreign country.

"It was almost like God was slamming the door in my face," he says, sitting the pandemic-era's requisite six feet from me in an office at the farm. Forming the third point of this conversational triangle is one of his daughters, Kayla Biegel, who manages Smits's farmers' market operations and handles social media. Carl is a lean, earnest, and accommodating man, open to even the most personal questions and unguarded in his answers. He also strikes me as complex: I can envision him in the collar he once contemplated, but also throwing elbows in the weekly church league basketball games that have been suspended during the pandemic. Kayla radiates positivity and youthful optimism. Let's be honest: When a New Yorker, and an agnostic one at that, visits with devout Christians far beyond a major city's limits, self-consciousness can seep in. That doesn't happen here. Carl and Kayla are gracious and genuine hosts, and our conversation is easy, intimate, and at times quite moving, as when Carl recounts the moment that his professional life turned the corner that led him here.

During Christmas break 1989 he had what might ironically be deemed an epiphany: Visiting his soon-to-be-wife Deb's family, he observed as her father, a farmer, and two brothers discussed a new state law banning yard waste from Illinois landfills.

In one swift burst of inspiration, Carl saw a possible calling: to take the yard waste, organic matter, that people were going to have to dispose of, use it as compost on a farm to invigorate the soil, and raise crops that could be sold in the city. He felt a pull, but, not hailing from a farming family, had no land, no knowledge, and no equipment. He'd be starting from scratch in a notoriously merciless profession with little room for error.

Deb had always told Carl she couldn't marry a farmer. She directed him to talk to her father, who tried to dissuade him for all the usual reasons: It's all-consuming, not lucrative, one cruel storm can ruin your season. But when Carl insisted he was being called to the land, rather than the ministry, his future father-in-law gave his blessing.

"I feel that I am being called to be a farmer, but I have no land, no equipment, no family in the farming business, and no experience to speak of running my own business," recalls Carl. "I was praying for God to show me where I should begin farming." He happened upon the twenty-nine acres of land that would become Smits Farms on Sauk Trail, an obsolete road in Chicago Heights, only because of a detour off Route 30, the main thoroughfare. A FOR SALE BY OWNER sign beckoned him, despite a portion of the property being overgrown with weeds and trees and populated by abandoned cars. He borrowed money from his father and "bought the farm" as he says with a laugh, from its owners, a couple in their eighties, the last living relatives of a family who had homesteaded the farm from the government in the 1800s. (When the couple learned that Carl planned to farm the land, rather than develop it into residential homes, they were overjoyed.)

In June 1990, he received his first truckload of yard waste. He had no equipment with which to spread it, and it reeked. "Think of your worst manure, and multiply it by ten," he says.

He knew he had to get it into the ground, where it would eventually do some good, so that August he purchased a small used tractor with a loader, and a small used manure spreader. Just when things were looking up, he received a severely worded cease-and-desist letter from Cook County, accusing him of operating a landfill without a permit and threatening a $25,000 *per*

Carl Smits and daughter Kayla Biegel standing
before the thyme used in our dish

day fine. (Carl theorizes that the aggressive stance was
motivated by there not being any law against stench, so
the only legal grounds for shutting him down was by
declaring his property a landfill, rather than a farm.)

Terrified though he was, with no savings and no
other options, Carl—just twenty-three at the time—
had no choice but to fight. (His business plan, such as it
was, was to survive on the revenue from the yard waste
for his first year.) He'd never had to enlist a lawyer before, so pleaded his case to a local counselor who took
pity on him, told Carl that if he did all the necessary
research, he'd accompany him to court and argue his

case. But things never got quite that far. When Carl and the attorney arrived at the courthouse in January 1991, they met with the state's attorney, then the judge, who dismissed the case.

The following year, with an eye on taking his wares to the burgeoning farmers' markets, Smits Farms began growing vegetables. (The property wasn't big enough for grain.)

Carl considers the early 1990s the golden years of Chicagoland farmers' markets. Suburban markets were in decline, but farmers were venturing into the city—a novelty. Firmly in the grip of the "buy local" movement, shoppers gobbled up whatever farmers had to offer. There were no sideshows like prepared food stalls, and farmers were purists, mostly growing whatever they brought to sell.

"The party action was at farmers' markets," says Carl. "You couldn't do anything wrong. No matter what you brought, you could set your price."

These days, in the winter, the large greenhouse stores everything from tractors to black plastic sheeting. But it's hardly an off-season: Sturdy herbs like rosemary and thyme, with relatively long growth cycles, are sown in pods in January and patiently nurtured until the first or second week of May, when Smits and his team are confident they've seen the last frost of the year. At that point, they're transplanted to the field: Artificially raised beds are produced with a shaping machine, and a water wheel—a metal wheel with a triangular protrusion that creates a divot with each rotation—is rolled over the beds. Water is poured into each hole, and a plug is dropped in. The water and soil produce a mud that, once dried, seals the plug into its new home. The first rosemary and thyme that go into the ground will be harvested in late June.

Kayla manages the harvesting schedule, directing a team that arrives each Tuesday morning at four-thirty. They take to the field and pick herbs by hand, getting down on their knees to do it. They clip the branches, then tie bunches together with rubber bands. The herbs are rinsed in the packing facility, then left to air-dry in the cooler until they are loaded onto trucks for farmers' markets. (Wherewithall actually purchases herbs from Smits at the Green City Market as needed, rather than having them delivered on a regular basis.)

I tell Carl that I'm struck that two of the farmers whose output feature in our dish had originally set out for the ministry.

"I don't want to be corny," I say, "but do you think there's anything to that, having to do with the Earth and caring for it?"

"I'm a Christian," he tells me. "I chose to plant the seed in a different way. I think the calling is real."

"Do you think this is what you were meant to do?"

"I do think I was meant to do this," he says. "I believe God calls people to do whatever He wants you to do. Whether that's a tendency or a literal thing, I totally believe that happens. I believe that you can be used no matter where you're at—whether you need a comforting word, or need to borrow a wrench . . . He doesn't just use ministers. He uses farmers' markets, chefs, farmers. *If* you're open to it, He's going to use you."

4

Preshift

Roughly an hour before the restaurant's doors opened, the kitchen and dining room teams gathered for two daily rituals: One was family meal. The other was preshift, referred to in some kitchens as *line-up* or simply *pre-service meeting*.

Preshift is the forum in which the dining room staff synchs up prior to receiving the first guests of the night. It can be likened to a theater troupe's pre-performance bonding exercises or to a police station's roll call. Led by Jessica, it takes place on the west side of the dining room, with the staff seated along the tables there. The meeting morphs from night to night. Tuesday, Jessica reviewed notes from Saturday night's service, and Tayler popped in and out to describe the week's dishes for the team as the cooks brought samples to the tables for them to taste. The servers took notes in their pads and José ran down the wines he's selected to pair with each course. On other nights, in addition to any special notes about guests and special occasions, missteps from the previous service are reviewed, discussed, and suggestions are made for how to avoid repeating them. Occasionally there will be a training exercise: Jessica might ask each server to say something descriptive about a dish on this week's menu. Or they might taste a wine and go around the horn, offering descriptors.

Staff meal tonight comprised steamed leftover cod, roasted beef, a salad, dressing, and assorted salsas. In addition to his prep tasks for nightly dinner service, family meal is Thomas's responsibility. Wherewithall's dinner menu derives from what's available from area farms; its staff meal derives from what's available *in house*—leftover ingredients, surplus dry goods, etc. On Tuesday, it was leftover chicken and eggplant, with a salad. Other nights might be a hodgepodge. Occasionally he'll purchase something inexpensive to bring a possible idea to fruition; for example, if all the makings of a great pasta are on hand, except for the pasta itself, he'll purchase some. Thomas delegates some staff meal prep tasks to the staff, especially Reuben, so it doesn't interfere too much with his day.

When the time comes, he arranges the components up on the pass and announces, "Staff's up!" Others fetch silverware, a beverage dispenser (with faucet)

Sous chef Thomas Hollensed keeps tabs on the
dining room with his signature system.

filled with ice water, glasses, and plates, then form a
chow line, serve themselves, and gather to eat together
along one of the banquettes.

Thomas grew up in Hattiesburg, Mississippi, a fifty-
four-square-mile city about one hundred ten miles
northeast of New Orleans. Since 1912, when the nick-
name was coined in a newspaper contest, it's been
known as "The Hub City," a nod to the concentration
of prominent rail lines that ran through it.

The son of two divorced professionals—his father, Hector, is an attorney; his mother, Tomi Ann, a nurse—Thomas confronted additional childhood challenges: In 1994, when he was five, his parents commenced their informal shared custody of him, and he received an ADHD diagnosis, a curiosity and stigma in Hattiesburg at the time. "I'm from Mississippi," Thomas says. "We're not the most progressive people in the world." Despite a string of tutors, Thomas frequently forgot to turn in homework assignments, and acted the class clown. He knows it was tough on his parents, especially his father, a respected member of the local business community who had traditional, conservative aspirations for his son. Doctors prescribed Thomas Ritalin, then Adderall, and finally Vyvanse, which he still takes today.

When he stopped growing, at age fifteen, his doctor blamed the medication, and prepared him to top out at five feet one. Father Hector insisted he take human growth hormone, which Thomas credits for another seven inches. He topped out at five feet eight. "Sometimes people joke that I'm short," Thomas beams. "I'm seven-foot as far as I'm concerned."

In a tumultuous young life during which his parents intermittently attempted a recoupling before permanently detaching, Thomas's touchstone was his paternal grandmother, Sara, who looked after him by day during summer breaks. A native of Quitman, Mississippi, in her eighties during Thomas's core childhood, she doted on him and he took full advantage: The pair regularly pigged out at Shoney's, a buffet chain, or at Thomas's favorite dining destination, Ward's, a family-owned chain of thirty-some locations scattered about southern Mississippi. His go-to feast there was two chili-cheese dogs and a Big One combo comprising a chili cheeseburger, French fries, and homemade root beer. (Decades later, it remains his death-row dinner.) More generally, he often gave in to a propensity for bingeing. At the local country club, he'd devour a grilled ham and cheese, chasing it with a burger at another food concession on the other side of the same building; he recalls eating as his favorite part of any day. He never doubted his parents' love but recognizes today that he was looking to food as a stand-in for something in those formative years.

He graduated from eater to cook the afternoon his grandmother decided to kill time by drafting him into a cooking project, roasting a chicken according to a recipe out of a spiral-bound Campbell's Soup–branded cookbook. As the bird roasted, the intergenerational tag team basted it with SunnyD orange juice until the internal temperature reached 220°F, a good fifty degrees beyond USDA guidelines. What emerged from the oven belonged more in a burn unit than on a dining table, but he remembers the activity fondly.

In time, his father remarried, to a woman named Marle (pronounced MAHR-lee), whose younger brother Evans lived with the family and was just eight years older than Thomas. Thomas looked up to Evans, a fraternity brother who epitomized college-boy cool, but to Evans (Thomas suspected) he was just Hector's screw-up kid.

Exasperated by Thomas's antics and failings, his family shipped him off to a succession of military boarding schools: Saint Stanislaus on the Mississippi coast, then Chamberlin-Hunt Academy, where empathy was tightly rationed. When he informed a dorm leader that the infirmary's supply of his ADHD medication had run out, rather than intervene, the leader outed him, scrawling on the cafeteria's whiteboard: *Thomas Hollensed needs Adderall and Prozac.* In his junior year, hobbled by a fractured femur that required him to hop around the grounds on crutches, he assumed he'd be exempt when his company was ordered to run to and from the road encircling the school property, as punishment for one member's clowning around.

"You, too, Hollensed," barked the leader. "*Crutch* to the road and back."

He complied, but also resolved to finagle his version of a Section 8 discharge, claiming a sudden and debilitating fear of climbing up and down stairs on crutches. Within weeks, the academy summoned his father to collect him.

Back home, during his senior year of high school Thomas took his first job, at The Bottling Company, built in 1915 in what is now Hattiesburg's Historic District. Occupying its own block, with a sunbeaten Coca-Cola logo splayed across its faded redbrick façade, it's now an events venue, especially for weddings. Thomas's grandmother had worked as a secretary in the building for thirty years, and his father worked the production line in summers during his boyhood. Now it was Thomas's turn.

Evans's best friend, Bottling Company general manager Brad Cornett, offered him the only open position, in the kitchen—Thomas's portal.

Removed from the family context, Evans took a liking to Thomas, functioning as a surrogate big brother at a delicate moment. Over the years after high school, Thomas failed out of a succession of colleges, but flourished at work. The Bottling Company served standard bar fare, but a kitchen is a kitchen, and he received an essential crash course in the basics, and just as essentially received long-denied positive reinforcement and validation. "From then, it blossomed," Thomas says. "It was just hamburgers . . . French fries. Fryer, blue plate type of stuff during the day. I got to skip the whole dishwasher-to-cook thing."

He also discovered an industrious streak, though not necessarily a virtuous one: After dark, The Bottling Company functioned as a nightclub, and Thomas as its gatekeeper carved out a side hustle by confiscating fake IDs and ransoming them for fifty dollars each.

"That's where I grew up," he says of the gig. "I essentially got the college experience [there]. I got to learn how to drink, how to go out, how to balance that with working. I was essentially the little brother of the bar."

It was heaven, an antidote to a young lifetime of academic foundering. It also introduced him to his wife, Brittany, whom he met in 2011 while tending bar at the Bottling Company's sister venue, Milk Shop. When she settled on University of Tennessee, Knoxville, as a graduate school for applied math, he followed her there and they moved in together.

A maturing influence, Brittany urged Thomas toward another run at college. He opted instead for culinary school, enrolling in a fledgling joint program between the University of Tennessee, Knoxville, and Pellissippi State Community College. Many of the students had been attracted by the adrenalized contrivances of reality-competition television shows, and were blindsided by the rigors and tedium of a real-world culinary education. Of the thirty-five who matriculated his year, only five survived to graduation. In a continuing reversal of his prior life experience, Thomas, animated by a classroom pursuit that engaged his imagination and enthusiasm, aced his coursework, earning a 4.0 grade point average his first semester. He sent a picture of his academic report to his father.

"For the longest time, a lot of stuff I did was for his approval," says Thomas. "If nothing else, it was a huge confidence booster."

After school, Thomas landed a plum job at Blackberry Farm, a destination resort with a high-end restaurant, in Walland, Tennessee. The restaurant functioned as his finishing school, taking his skills to the next level. When he and Brittany relocated to Chicago, like many members of Wherewithall's 2021 crew Thomas secured a position at Parachute before the pandemic. When his mother dined there, and witnessed him flourishing as sous chef, she cried. His father's subsequent visit was more subdued, but Thomas could see it in his face: "He's proud of me," he says. "He brags about me all the time."

Back in our Saturday night service, it's about ten minutes past nine o'clock. Thomas and Reuben complete a plate-up of eight fish dishes, two of which Nooshâ delivers to Table 12, whose next course will be *our* dish.

Jon Templin standing before one of his greenhouses

As soon as those dishes are up on the pass, Reuben scoops up the Lexan holding picked sorrel leaves and heads downstairs to the walk-in to replenish it for the remainder of the evening.

"When you first said you were going to come, I was kind of freaking out."

That's Jon Templin, proprietor of Butternut Sustainable Farm, a twelve-acre concern just outside Sturgis, Michigan, where those sorrel leaves were grown. I feel terrible. After all, I *want* to see his farm in its natural state.

"I was like, *Oh, I've got to clean up this, and I've got to clean up that*. And then I thought you want to see what we actually *are*. I was having a little bit of panic, and I finally said, *No!*"

I exhale, thankful that he had let himself off the hook.

"It's a little messier than the other farms," he continues, as he begins to show me around. "But it's all part of what we do."

Jon is talking about Butternut's unkempt appearance, which if I'm honest, does read like one man's agricultural paean to the randomness of the universe. If he has an ego, it manifests in ways other than order. The farm comprises patches of wild growth, with all manner of plants and weeds tangled with and encroaching on each other, all of it intentional.

"I like to have things more natural," he says. "A lot of farms, it's all just straight-line plants, no weeds, no nothing. But that kills the biodiversity. And I think it's really important to have biodiversity, because not all weeds are bad. We don't want to hurt the production of our plants, but we also don't want to take too much time to take out some of the stuff that necessarily isn't bad."

The approach works. From this disheveled spot on Route 147, less than half a mile from Sauger Lake, Jon and his small team nurture produce that

pleases even Chicago's most notoriously perfectionist chefs. Grant Achatz, the wizard behind modernist
Oz, Alinea, all but monopolizes Butternut's tomato
supply. This is especially ironic because Achatz's
methods rely on exactitude: ingredients are measured
to the gram, ovens and circulators set to the degree,
and seconds of cooking time tracked as closely as an
Olympic sprinter's. But his tomatoes grow within a
ragtag collection of M.A.S.H. unit–like greenhouses
where one must scavenge for them like Easter eggs
among the greenery.

Jon founded Butternut Sustainable Farm in 2012,
but his family has farmed the land on which it's situated for four generations. (The house where Jon grew
up still stands at one end of the property.) Jon studied
agro-ecology at Indiana's Goshen College and his interest in sustainable farming was sparked during a summer
at Merry Lea Environmental Learning Center's Reith
Village, an ecological field station, also affiliated with
Goshen College.

Not unlike Lloyd Nichols, Carl Smits, and James
Lester, and despite his formal agricultural education,
much of Jon's approach derives from trial and error,
intuition and experimentation. Like Lloyd Nichols, he
raises a head-spinning variety of crops—walking the
comparatively small property, he points out everything
from tomatoes to cucumbers to eggplant to I-don't-

know-how-many varieties of chile peppers to straw-
berries and ground cherries. He doesn't specialize in
herbs, but he grows plenty of them, too, ranging from
lemon balm to oregano to summer savory and perilla.

The cycle of life spins endlessly here. On this August
morning, patches from which spring kohlrabi, Swiss
chard, and lettuces have been harvested, are washed
out, their square-yardage overgrown with weeds, while
a few feet away, a future planting area awaits tilling
and seeding. Jon's crew actually tilled it a week prior,
but the weekend brought three inches of rain, necessi-
tating a redo.

"The climate has been very erratic in the last five
years," he laments. "And it's been a lot harder to plan
because we're not having gradual changes like we used
to. This year's been all rain. It goes from super dry to
super wet, and nothing in between." This volatility
demands real-time adjustments, with a slight margin
provided by the one hundred fifty different crops. Any
failed crops still represent wasted time and work, but if
one goes down, others will see the farm through.

Jon doesn't do much research about farming practices, preferring instead to arrive at his own personal
farming style through observation and trial and error.
It sounds radical, but is it? He doesn't put anything
harmful in the earth or on the plants, and so it can

be easily argued that the only test that matters is how what's grown here eats.

The farm's breakout star is its tomatoes, which have been feted in the press. (*Chicago* magazine called them "the most sought-after tomatoes in the Midwest.") During peak season, the team will pack about one hundred ten-pound boxes of tomatoes bound for city restaurants each week. Much of Butternut's revenue also derives from what Jon calls "edible flowers and garnishy-type things." Nasturtiums alone account for thousands of dollars in revenue weekly.

Like every farm that mainly supplies restaurants, Butternut is still licking its wounds from the pre-vaccine COVID era. Even the pivot to take-out didn't offer a market for items like edible flowers, and not just because they suddenly seemed frivolous. "You can't put a nasturtium in a to-go box because it's just going to wilt," Jon says.

On the other hand, during peak COVID, the weekender population of the surrounding towns mushroomed, as well-to-do Chicagoans and Detroiters (Sturgis is roughly equidistant from both) able to work via Zoom blew into town happy to spend tens of thousands of dollars above asking price—*cash*—for second homes where they could sit out the plague and cool themselves with lake breezes. Previously, local

Butternut Sustainable Farm field workers pick ground cherries by hand.

customers gravitated to basics like green cucumbers and red tomatoes; these newbies, accustomed to dining at upscale restaurants, showed up to Butternut's Saturday farmstand in fancy cars, eager to shell out for striped heirloom tomatoes and unfamiliar vegetables with which they could play chef. As of July 2021, the farm was experiencing weekly growth and Jon had his eye on converting the CSA business to farmstand.

In normal times, Butternut's most prized tomatoes sell for $4.50 per pound. That sounds exorbitant, but these are not bit players fated to be diced up and sautéed for the base of a sauce or braising liquid. Butternut's fruits and vegetables are marquee divas, starring in dishes whose success depends on their superior flavor. Butternut grades some of its most in-demand produce according to a signature hierarchy: Its famed tomatoes, for example, are designated *firsts*, *seconds*, or *thirds*. Firsts flirt with perfection—spherical and essentially unblemished; restaurants will not cook these, but rather serve them in some fashion that fetishizes their tomato-ness. Seconds might display a divot or flaw near the stem, or they may be too small or large for elegance, even if sliced; these usually wind up in the confines of a sandwich. Thirds are misshapen, perhaps even ridged, dooming them to the blender or food processor, where they may be whirred into gazpacho or then strained to produce tomato water.

In Butternut Sustainable Farm's temporal universe, Wednesday—delivery day—is the sun around which the other days revolve. On that morning, Jon himself revs up his truck in the late morning and drives the roughly two and a half hours to Chicago, where he makes the rounds of his restaurant clients, bringing them the ingredients he's nurtured from the seed or sapling stage.

Every Monday, the crew checks on large crops to see if they grew unruly over the weekend, picking tomatoes and cucumbers before they can become unwieldy—they also start to die as soon as they reach maximum size.

The sorrel leaves that adorn our dish grow in the shade of poke leaves.

Butternut is small potatoes compared to a sprawling generational farm like Nichols. Accordingly, Jon employs just a handful of workers, mostly local high school and college kids. Unlike many farmers, he refuses to hire—and reap the economic benefits of hiring—undocumented immigrants. "One of the biggest things I believe is that sustainable farming is not just taking care of the environment, but the business in full. Being good and paying a fair wage is an important part of that business model."

Commitments such as that contribute to the price of foodstuffs, which is reflected in what restaurants charge for a dish, or a meal. Sometimes small farmers and producers incur expenses simply due to their relatively meager purchasing power; for example, Louis-John Slagel pays significantly more for boxes than his corporate competitors, who purchase in bulk and receive heavily discounted prices in return. Restaurants that choose to support and source from local farmers often put themselves at a competitive disadvantage because their prices seem out of whack with those of restaurants that stock their walk-ins with less expensive and often less fresh and pristine proteins and produce from national companies or discount restaurant warehouses.

Ordering is simple: A list is emailed to restaurant clients no later than 5:00 P.M. Saturday. The criteria for a crop's inclusion on the list is that it be plentiful enough that if every restaurant ordered it in a given week, he could fulfill every order. If the yield of something recedes, as anise did this week, he'll omit it and hold off on reinstating it until the next growth.

Some restaurants receive standing deliveries week to week. From others, orders roll in day and night almost as soon as the list is circulated, either by return email, a separate email, or text. They are scribbled in dry-erase marker on a whiteboard fixed to the wall of a modest concrete hut set amid the growing lots, which serves as the packing facility. Every morning, Jon adds orders that have rolled in overnight to the board, which dictates what the crew will pick that day; before heading out to a patch, each team member will scribble their initials next to the item, signaling to others that someone's on it, which also prevents double picking. When an order's been fulfilled and packaged with a label and date, Jon highlights it in yellow, then in blue once it goes into a restaurant's individual delivery cooler.

Monday, Tuesday, and Wednesday are the longest, most taxing days. What can be picked ahead of time gets picked ahead of time and stored in a walk-in refrigerator in the packing facility. (The facility illustrates a universal truth of independent farms: They will find a way to use or repurpose any and all mechanical and electronic devices and machines. Here, a past-its-prime washing machine has been fit with a large plastic basket and is used to spin greens dry; the climate-controlled walk-in at one end of the facility is cooled by a window-unit air conditioner that's been positioned in a cut-out portion of the wall and jury-rigged to "trick" it into running constantly and keeping the temperature lower than it's intended to.) But orders keep coming until the stated deadline of 7:00 A.M. Tuesday and, chefs being chefs, some will trickle in after that, and Jon'll do what he can to make it happen, even sending a crew into the field just before the truck departs for the city.

Butternut sells by the pound and packs its produce into bags. It's a financially altruistic gesture of sustainability: Many restaurants reflexively order cases, so they are prone to surpluses that end up in staff meal, or the bin. Jon's way, a restaurant might order, say, seven pounds of cucumbers, which isn't much. But there's no waste, and Jon would rather sell less than oversell.

On Wednesday and Thursday, the team picks for CSA boxes and for the handful of restaurants Butternut services in Kalamazoo and South Bend.

On Thursday and Friday, Jon and his team tend to the farm, readying it for the following week. Occasionally they make a second trip to the city on those days, to replenish herbs or other items for a few customers. They also regularly return to the city a second time in late summer's peak tomato season.

Sunday, there's just one employee in rotation, a woman who picks squash and cucumbers all day because both can grow *inches* overnight.

Like James Lester a little ways upstate, Jon's not-unique belief is that plants have to stress and strain to produce superior fruits and vegetables. To put this in human terms, adversity reveals character, or perhaps develops it. Jon himself employs wine as an easy example, citing Italian red varietal grapevines that must wriggle their way out of harsh volcanic soil, resulting in well-structured juice. Accordingly, this kind, gentle man deprives his fruits and vegetables: "We barely give the tomato [plants] any water once they start putting out tomatoes."

A tangential philosophy of laissez-faire affords those weeds clemency. Many farmers pride themselves on perfectly geometric gardens. Butternut's unkempt appearance can be a shock to visitors—professional colleagues and hobbyist gardeners alike might blanch at the sight of a single weed, let alone an outbreak. The same was once true of Jon, but he's over that, and has conditioned himself not to mind.

Toward the residential end of the property stands a cluster of hoop houses—steel frameworks over which hang plastic sheeting that can be elevated or lowered like window blinds to encourage or deflect wind flow. The shelter isn't meant to provide warmth but rather to elude moisture: Jon, whose background is in biology, stops watering and feeding the tomato plants after the spring, though he does tend their soil to moderate disease.

"Most farms are worried about their yields. We don't get the greatest yields, but we're getting a far better product where we can charge more," he says. "And our customers are the ones that want that sort of thing. A lot of the Michelin stars, a lot of the James Beard chefs—those are the people that we work with."

We encounter our dish's sorrel in the shade of enormous poke leaves that shadow it, aiding its growth.

The farm doesn't sell poke—the berries that will grow on it over time are poisonous—but Jon permits it in the name of biodiversity, and for that precious shade. When the berries come, the team will trim them back.

Jon breaks off a sorrel leaf and hands it to me. I bite off half and my taste buds light up with a shock of lemon, the same one that brought an unexpected acidic undercurrent to our dish when I first tasted it.

Sustainable is a curious buzzword that ten different people—even food professionals—might define in ten different ways. It connotes local, pesticide free, ecologically responsible food, but its *Oxford English Dictionary* definition is, simply, "able to be maintained at a certain rate or level."

"For me, sustainability is a holistic view of the business," says Jon, who feels strongly enough about it that he's made it part of his farm's name. "It's taking care of your employees, taking care of your customers, taking care of the products, producing something that's beautiful. We're taking from the earth, basically, but—this sounds hippie-dippie—we're trying to put back."

That means making decisions like laying on literal tons of compost every year, leaving weeds for the bees, and sparing inedible flowers. He grabs a fistful of milkweed as we stroll the farm. "Like all this here: I just let it grow for the monarch butterflies. Leaving things in a place that creates a natural habitat, but also you're getting production out of it at the same time."

Proximity to the lake limits the number of frosts that test the farm each winter, and creates a microclimate that's dry relative to South Bend and Kalamazoo. The snow band ends about fifteen miles away, and summer storms tend to leapfrog Sturgis, which is fine by Jon.

"Too much water can be worse than dry conditions," he says. "We have the ability to water."

Small-scale independent farms, like the restaurant industry many of them serve, are high risk. "Something like six out of eight farms like this go out of business after five years," Jon says. Before COVID, the farm—in its eighth year—was nudging the fiscal needle toward the black, but the pandemic was merciless. Government assistance sustained the operation, including paying key employees to whom Jon delegated quotidian tasks. Meanwhile, he holed up in the house, developing more efficient and profitable systems for the future: his agricultural swing for the reset.

Also, Jon's passion—like that of his counterparts in restaurants—offers scant downtime and insufficient pay and benefits, and exacts a physical toll. Some seeds go in the ground as early as February and the earth gives back produce right through to December, so January offers the only opportunity for extended rest. And because his business and staffing are seasonal, in the supposed slowdown of winter, he takes most of the work on himself.

In the summer, Jon employs about seven full-time workers. The hours are irregular, except for the start time: Everyone clocks in at 7:00 A.M., and nobody leaves until the day's work is done. Quitting time can be 7:00 P.M. or as late as midnight, especially on Tuesday, with the city deliveries the next day. (On that day, everyone arrives at 6:00 A.M.)

Jon makes his own deliveries, notching about twenty stops everywhere from chef Erick Williams's Virtue Restaurant & Bar on the South Side, to Logan Square on the north, and everywhere in between. The regular face time with the chefs presents an opportunity to glean any feedback about product or practices, and prod them for as much information as possible about what they're looking for—stem length, color, sizing, and more. If he can find it or grow it at the farm, he'll make it happen.

Delivering personally also gives Jon a chance to go over that week's produce with the chef. For example, at Wherewithall, Tayler will direct him to a clean spot on the pass where he'll lay out the cooler's contents, giving Tayler a chance to inspect it. This is also when he might alert her to any timely information, such as if an impending storm is likely to cause a shortage of a particular ingredient the following week.

He also enjoys talking with chefs because he's a closet whisk himself. "Everyone says I should have been a chef," he tells me. "But I don't want to do something that I enjoy doing to relax, as a profession. So this gives me a way that I can do something that's involved in the industry, but not necessarily where I'm cooking every day."

I ask Jon what kind of food he'd cook in the restaurant of his dreams: modernist constructs like Grant Achatz's, or something more rustic?

"Simple, rustic," he says. "Let the vegetables talk. That's one of the things I love here: I can walk out and get any ingredient I want and make whatever I want."

5

Service

At Wherewithall, service continues to ratchet up, this Saturday night delivering on the promise of its reservation count. At the end of the pass, Tayler pans the kitchen area, monitoring the progress of Jenna, Reuben, and Thomas through various stages of the courses they're readying.

A few parties arrived late tonight, adding to the pressure on the kitchen. Tayler's doing what she can to keep her crew moving and prevent a pileup, both in the kitchen and at the podium when more guests arrive for their reservations. The playlist helps keep things chill with Fruit Bat's shaggy "Humbug Mountain Song."

"Auto-fire apps when the broth is walking," she tells Thomas. Translation: "Don't wait for me. When bowls of broth leave the pass for a table, get Reuben going on the appetizer course for the corresponding party."

Tayler Ploshehanski pitches in on the pass during service.

Thomas nods, wipes his brow with his forearm, takes a swig from his water bottle and a deep breath. Shit's getting real.

So many courses are in so many stages of preparation that unless you are personally working a station, it's impossible to decipher exactly what is going on at each one. There's not a burner, oven rack, or square inch of counter space that isn't spoken for. The cooks don't stop moving, unless it's to quickly survey everything in their care and remember what needs their attention next and most urgently. The entire scene, playing out just a few feet from where diners are reveling, is the very picture of stress. And yet, if you pay close attention, every once in a while you'll catch one of the cooks smiling to themselves. This is what they live for.

Johnny is alongside Tayler at the pass. For the moment, it's best for him to lean back. There's no room on the hot line for another body, and Tayler's in good, flowing communication with her team.

Even at this delicate moment, responsibility for quality control also rests with Tayler. And so she gives real-time feedback, as when she notes a discrepancy among the cuts of hake on plates bound for the same table. "Some of those are too thin," she tells Thomas, who nods his receipt of the message.

Chef de cuisine, or CDC, is a coveted position in most restaurants, conferring creative authority without the insomniac preoccupations of ownership. There are tradeoffs: Customarily, the media spotlight trains on the chef-owner(s), which can seed resentment in CDCs. But Tayler's shy. Has been since elementary school, where she trembled so badly whenever required to stand and deliver that teachers invited her to present to them privately after class. The issue, it turned out years later, stemmed from difficulty reading that was ameliorated when she belatedly discovered that she'd needed glasses all along. By that time, self-consciousness had taken hold. Tayler no longer *suffers*—watching her brief the dining room team on this week's menu, you'd assume at least average confidence—but neither does she crave the invitations and opportunities for which peers wage all-out campaigns: television gigs, culinary conference speaking slots, or even being interviewed for or featured in a book.

As with many colleagues—at Wherewithall, throughout Chicago, and around the world—Tayler's career is something of an accident, or at least a Plan B, C, or D. That's not to say that, again as with so many kitchen siblings, there weren't signs along the way: Growing up in Hampshire, Illinois, Tayler helped her mom make dinner, baked cookies with her grandmother, and pressed sleepover guests into baking projects. At Christmas, she pitched in on the family pierogi production line and assisted in fashioning Polish holiday staples from scratch. Yet she never considered the possibility of going pro.

The village of Hampshire occupies roughly ten square miles, northwest of Elgin and about sixty miles northwest of Chicago. In Tayler's formative years, Hampshire was unincorporated. Rural. Country. Some details all but dare urbanites to resist relating them with the cadence of a punch line. For example: If you or a loved one were gruesomely wounded, in the throes of cardiac arrest, or fleeing a flame-engulfed building, to summon emergency services . . . you had to first dial "0," and then ask the operator to please connect you to 911. Sometimes even natives can't help but laugh: While I was observing prep one afternoon at Wherewithall, Tayler and Thomas bonded over their respective small-town upbringings, one-upping each other with a succession of hometown quirks. Tayler cinched victory by recounting an annual occasion at her high school: Bring Your Tractor to School Day.

She was born Tayler Stecker. Her parents moved the family—Tayler and two older sisters—into the house she would grow up in before her first birthday. Her father, a cement mason since age fifteen, was the family's sole earner, supplementing his full-time job with side gigs, notching between eighty and one hundred hours of physical labor per week. He was bodily present at home, but a daily 4:30 A.M. wake-up time and marathon of physical labor required him to turn in immediately after dinner.

Money was tight, so the Stecker girls entertained themselves by biking and fishing, catching bullfrogs at a nearby pond, and probing neighboring houses' window wells for toads and salamanders. Once a year, the family took a camping vacation.

What kind of kid was she?

"It's a hard question for me," she says, sitting across from me at Table 10, the one closest to the kitchen, which functions as an unofficial, unwalled staff conference table by day. "I wasn't stupid in any way, but reading gave me trouble and I was insecure about it. Other than that, I was kind of outgoing, silly."

Early on Saturday morning, July 24 (the day that leads into the service that's the subject of this book), Tayler picks me up in her black Chevy Equinox so I can tag along with her to Green City Market, where she'll meet Thomas to replenish some ingredients for the last service of the week. We rumble through deserted early-morning Chicago streets, Willie Nelson's 1973 album *Shotgun Willie* twanging on the sound system. It occurs to me that for all of Tayler's big-city success (just about a week prior, Eater Chicago, the restaurant news, gossip, and feature website, profiled her), we're only fifty miles from where she grew up, and she retains the social mores trained into her there. (This is not uncommon in Chicago's culinary circle, which draws much of its citizenry from rural Illinois and surrounding states such as Michigan, Ohio, Kentucky, and Indiana.) At the market, unlike native urbanites, she makes no clumsy effort to ingratiate herself with the farmers: She's chummy with those she knows and likes, but when one farm's attendant flatly refuses to accommodate a common billing request, Tayler flash-freezes her out as if they'd been high school nemeses. She's also retained a provincial modesty; driving from the market to Wherewithall, she calls back to our conversation earlier in the week, when she'd told me she didn't have any hobbies or pastimes as a kid. Something about being around all those farmers caused her to reconsider the answer.

"I mean, where I grew up, you're not supposed to brag," she says. "But I did things—snowboarding, hunting, fishing." She also played organized softball until age seventeen, says she was a good batter, and able to toggle between outfield and second base on defense.

After graduating high school, she drifted through a semester twenty miles from home at Northern Illinois University in Dekalb where, surfing a natural aptitude for math, she started down a business accounting path. But it didn't take. She'd earned As and Bs in high school but hated the college environment and underperformed. It was about this time that she felt the first disconcerting tug of the tractor beam that can lock in on small-town girls as they mature, dragging them toward a random vocation (hairstyling on the other side of her mind's sliding doors) or the altar–maternity ward express lane. She's uncomfortable voicing this: Plenty of her friends and peers chose that life, and she thinks it's a fine one. But she wanted something different for herself. She tried photography classes at Elgin Community College, decided she lacked visual instincts or flair, and crossed that off her mental list. Nutrition courses piqued her interest, but she didn't have the requisite credits to take up the subject at University of Illinois Chicago. Still, the notion, combined with her deft home cooking, prompted her boyfriend at the time to open the portal for her by suggesting culinary school. In 2011, at age twenty-two, she matriculated at Kendall College. Far as she was concerned, her career path was set, and the ease with which she picked up knife skills and other fundamentals in her first weeks at Kendall offered all the reinforcement she needed.

For her externship, Tayler secured one of two coveted spots at Blackbird, the first restaurant by chef Paul Kahan and his partner Donnie Madia, who jointly went on to found the prolific One Off Hospitality Group. At Blackbird, she met David Posey, the chef who became her first and primary mentor. Often this relationship transcends the term of employment. Any cook will call their higher-up at a given time "Chef," but some teacher-mentee bonds may last a lifetime, not unlike a parent-child relationship. And just as adults may refer to their parents as "Mom" and "Dad" for life, full-fledged chefs will continue to address their mentor(s) as "Chef" for the rest of their days. (Without meaning to culturally appropriate, I've long believed that *chef*, when meant in this way, would be well replaced by the East Asian honorific *sensei*, with its combined meanings and connotations of elder, expert, and educator, and its application across a broad spectrum of disciplines.)

A culinary student's initial foray into a professional kitchen compares—minus the life-and-death consequences—to the vault from boot camp to combat, or from flight simulator to passenger jet; the chasm between theoretical and actual is vast. How smoothly a newbie transitions is a dependable predictor of their long-term compatibility with the work and the life. Tayler acclimated quickly, to both the demands of that specific kitchen and the real-world stakes of cooking for paying customers. Blackbird's kitchen team at the time was a fledgling band of future all-stars, like the cast of *Parks and Recreation* or the Jon Stewart–era stable of *The Daily Show* correspondents. Many who then anonymously toiled on the line today own businesses in myriad states, to varying success: Jennifer Kim (who now runs Chicago's Alt[ernative] Economy) helped train Tayler, who also worked alongside Ryan Pfeiffer (now chef-proprietor of Big Kids, a Chicago sandwich shop walking distance from Wherewithall) and Kyle Cottle (now chef de cuisine of Sepia).

For reasons that are perhaps unknowable, most fledgling cooks develop an animal affinity for one or more specific tasks; Tayler gravitated to cleaning delicate ingredients—peeling dainty burlap-colored chanterelle mushrooms by waving her paring knife over them, or judiciously employing the knife to excavate sweetbreads, relieving them of their membranes and veins.

Participating in the action of a dinner service wasn't promised to Blackbird's interns; Tayler's contemporary there never was summoned from the bench. But Tayler was, including on Saturday nights, when the kitchen pumped out one hundred fifty covers. She was assigned to *garmo*, also called *amuse* at Blackbird, the entry-level service position in most kitchens. Tayler found the environment supportive but tough. Novices were patiently shown what to do, then expected to pull their weight. In her first hours on the line, sensing Posey scrutinizing her every move, her hands shook. "Just breathe," the cooks whispered. In time, she was charged with executing dishes from start to finish, including sweetbreads; poached, chilled prawns, served cold with chanterelle mushrooms, burnt onions, and nutmeg cream; and a lamb tartare for which she cleaned and cut lamb saddles.

"I think being in that type of kitchen right off the rip helped toughen my skin up," says Tayler. "I didn't realize it then, but I do now: They trusted me."

David Posey is a tall, brooding chef, thickly built, with the stubbly beard and blunt facial features of a rugby player. He exhibits a verbal stinginess that many—including Tayler's husband, Peter Ploshehanski, a fellow whisk who once worked for Posey—initially find gruff and intimidating. The daughter-father dynamic of her childhood—in addition to an innate reticence, her father grappled with depression and anxiety—enabled her to perceive something different: "I saw quiet reserve," she says. "I don't think it made me nervous or uncomfortable to be around someone like that. I'm not super chatty when I'm working. David's a little socially awkward. I'm a little socially awkward. We get each other."

Tayler wanted to learn butchery, badly enough that she'd come in on days off.* Like a fledgling serial killer, she started with small animals—rabbits and ducks. When she felt ready, she told Posey she wanted to learn how to break down a whole animal, a big ask of any busy chef, but Tayler felt she understood something about Posey: "He was harsh but also super caring and patient. If you show interest in something, he's going to make sure you get to do it."

"Alright," the chef said, then uttered an order suitable for enshrinement on a T-shirt: "Go get your goat."

---

* A motivated young cook spending "unclocked" time at a place of employment to pick up new information and skills was, until recently, a long-standing tradition in restaurants. Today, in the United States, it's illegal to work without pay, regardless of the employee's desire, which limits what a cook can physically do during uncompensated hours.

(At the time, the restaurant was butchering goats in-house for a confit dish.) This is how knowledge is passed down in the pro cooking trade, even among people who attended culinary school. On Tuesday afternoon at Wherewithall, Johnny showed Thomas how to break down and trim strip loin. On Wednesday, Tayler interrupted Thomas's prep to help him further hone his technique, demo-ing how to pull the silver skin *really tight* and keep it taut as she ran a knife in longer, smoother strokes than he had been along the beef to remove the skin with minimal meat attached to it.

Tayler's cohort at Kendall was close-knit—a female-dominant group who deliberately stuck together to offset the overwhelmingly male class composition. Following their internships, they returned to school and spent about two months at The Dining Room at Kendall College, its student-run eatery.

This was where, a decade before she was hired as Wherewithall's chef de cuisine, she first met its future co-chef and co-owner Beverly Kim, a slight Korean American, thirty-three at the time, herself a graduate of Kendall. Beverly devised the restaurant's menu and set the rules, and the team executed, rotating kitchen stations every few days. Students also conceived and ran their own specials. Tayler and her girlfriends took an instant liking to Beverly but also found her overly serious, wanting to loosen her up, be her pal. In truth, Beverly has a goofy side, and an explosive, joy-filled laugh, but didn't unleash it until late in the term.

To her students, Beverly was a budding talent who had paid her dues and was at the threshold of the promised land of chef-ownership. In reality, she and Johnny were bleeding out financially and desperate for whatever infusion they could obtain, even a culinary instructor's meager compensation.

But first, the backstory: Beverly traces her initial attraction to cooking to childhood. Her mother, devoted to raising her children and keeping the family home, prepared an American dinner *and* a Korean dinner nightly. The youngest, by nearly a decade, of four sisters in a brotherless household—a fact that pained her parents, especially her father—Beverly gravitated to her mother's side, functioning as a sous chef by having ingredients and implements at the ready. Her mother was known among their community for her discerning palate and superb culinary technique. The Kims didn't pay their children an allowance, so Beverly came to regard cooking as a way of showing her friends affection by baking—rather than *buying*—them gifts.

Her parents' sexism was matched at school by persistent racism and stereotyping, like the teacher who informed her that she'd be graded to a higher standard because "her people" were able to memorize letters better than the average American. Beverly concluded that the teacher was confusing Korean culture for Chinese.* (Beverly was born in the United States and English was her first language.)

"I feel like there's this foreignness about being born Asian or Korean that people don't understand or educate themselves [about]," she says. "I think maybe her intention was really out of a good place, but it could be harmful if you're propagating information that's not correct, and not understanding what being American really is. We're all settlers here, you know?"

In retrospect, she sees the same silver lining around her teacher's stereotyping and her parents' chauvinism: Both manifested pernicious and systemic falsehoods that enabled her to empathize with myriad people she's encountered, personally and professionally.

That all would come later. At the time, she was just a kid who loved to cook. A loosely defined extra-credit assignment for a junior high French class afforded an early glimmer of future ambition: To earn the extra credit, she devised and executed a three-course French dinner, going full-on restaurant by preparing haricots

---

* In his book *Outliers*, Malcolm Gladwell offers several linguistic and practical reasons for Chinese children's superior ability to memorize long number chains.

verts, chicken chasseur, and chocolate mousse; thoughtfully selecting plates; and stitching together a music mix to set the mood. "I just had fun," she giggles today. "Cooking and the whole process of hospitality is *fun*."

Like many Korean—and more generally, *Asian*—families who had migrated to the United States, the Kims harbored white-collar aspirations for their progeny. Beverly connects this to *han*, a Korean word that describes a sort-of righteous indignation, or sorrowful rage, born of the country's past colonization by Japan. Her own sensation of *han* was stoked by her father's open disappointment in her gender: Being the fourth daughter born to Korean parents was an indignity, the latest child incapable of maintaining the family's name, a stigma magnified by Beverly's father being the only male in his generation of the family.

It wasn't Beverly herself, but her sister Lee Ann, who—having observed the gravitational pull the kitchen had on her—first suggested she consider cooking as a vocation. At sixteen, Beverly took an internship at The Ritz-Carlton, Chicago, working under chef Sarah Stegner, one of the city's culinary community's elder statespeople, currently co-owner and operator of Prairie Grass Cafe in Northbrook, Illinois. Beverly considered enlisting in the military as a cook—even met with an Army recruiter—then was accepted to Northwestern University. There was just one problem: The Kims' bank balance had been drained by Papa Kim's business transitioning to HMOs, a losing proposition for private practitioners, and his having put three other daughters through college and financed a few of their weddings. Both parents balked at the notion that they'd cover tuition at Northwestern, where Beverly wanted to study—of all the useless things—*French*. They salted the wound by footnoting their refusal that they'd have scrounged up the necessary funds had she been a young man. One of her father's comments at the time still irks her today: "If you were my son, I would kick your ass for going to culinary school, but since you're a daughter, I do think you can at the very least be a good wife because you would make your family happy." The sentiment represents what Beverly considers "old, old Korean thinking."

Han struck again: Beverly resolved to fend for herself and prove them woefully wrong. She holds the opposite view of cooking, regarding it as a practical, even conservative, pursuit. In exchange for two years of school (the typical length of a culinary education program), you acquired a trade that was portable and always in demand. She considered applying to The Culinary Institute of America. But Stegner, who was fast becoming Beverly's *sensei*, talked her out of it, recommending Kendall College—local and less expensive. (For all her success, Beverly regrets denying herself the college experience of

Beverly Kim speaking to the team during a weekly managers meeting

a traditional liberal arts school.) In those preenlighten-ment days, even cooking school was defined by "locker room talk, machismo, masochistic behavior, that was all kind of normal back then," she says. Diminishing or degrading women was commonplace. "I had to learn how to have a thick skin about it because it bothered me. It doesn't say anything about Kendall; it was the culture. Back then it wasn't as PC." The open chauvinism caused her to periodically question whether she had chosen the right career. But she soldiered on.

Beverly is unfailingly polite, slightly built, and so bereft of body fat that it's easy to imagine one of the Windy City's signature gusts lifting her off her feet.

But she's no pushover. She didn't adopt her parents' devout religiosity, but does consider herself spiritual. She believes that obstacles are dropped in one's path for a reason, which may lead to a purpose. For her, it's meant redirecting her pain and suffering at being *the other* in various scenarios to helping people. She and Johnny have lent their time, life force, names, and restaurants to a variety of causes. Most prominently, they co-founded The Abundance Setting, a nonprofit that supports working mothers in the hospitality industry, where nocturnal working hours, often-minuscule wages and benefits, and the physical toll of the work itself can make both maternity and career seem like Sisyphean enterprises.

After Kendall, Beverly worked for Charlie Trotter at his internationally famous eponymous restaurant. Trotter, who died in 2013 at just fifty-four, ranked among the most mercurial American chefs in a generation rife with them. A child of privilege, he developed his skills in a rapid-fire procession of more than two dozen kitchens around the country and the world. Back home in Chicago, he opened his destination restaurant in a converted townhouse in 1987. It quickly established itself as one of the most ambitious restaurants in the United States, as well as a groundbreaking one, introducing vegetable tasting menus alongside more traditional ones. Trotter himself, it was well known, could be affectionate and generous, or ice-cold and vicious, sometimes to the same person, within the same hour. (He also devoted considerable time and resources to a variety of charities.)

Beverly found the Trotter's environment stifling and excessively, unnecessarily stressful. For example, as a daily exercise, she was expected to prepare a dish for the chef at exactly 1 P.M. This was on top of her other work, and often when she was finished, Trotter was nowhere to be found. Many co-workers ate up these ostensibly developmental aspects of life at the restaurant, but Beverly came to consider them superfluous. She also found the culture elitist and boy's clubby, likening it to a culinary Harvard. At one point, to diminish her femininity in hopes of fitting in and putting herself on a war footing, she went full-on *G.I. Jane,* chopping off her hair.

Employees at Trotter's were paid a shift wage, and expected to work well beyond what would, by any standard, be considered normal working hours, without overtime compensation. This was common industry practice, the rationale being that you were learning a craft that would help you advance, perhaps eventually to chefdom. But it didn't compute for Beverly, given Trotter's well-known wealth. "I couldn't believe how sweatshop it was compared to how much money he had," she says.

In 2003, Beverly did the unthinkable. She spearheaded a federal class-action lawsuit against Trotter
seeking unpaid overtime. If Johnny and Beverly per-
sonify a shifting American kitchen culture, this was
one of the demarcation lines between "old" and "new."
Trotter's preeminence in the Chicago dining universe at
the time was absolute. Even today, a professional Trotter
family tree overhangs the city's dining community—
many of its most acclaimed restaurants are run by
alumni of his kitchens or graduates of the alumni's
kitchens.

The lawsuit was settled in 2005. Trotter parted with
more than $700,000 to workers who prepared food in
his restaurant between 1998 and 2002. (Had all eligible
employees signed onto the suit, it would have cost
him substantially more.) The action also cost Beverly:
In kitchens around town, and on the record in articles
in print and online, Trotter disciples took a rhetorical
crowbar to her, painting her as soft, a crybaby, and metabolically unqualified for the life. "I had the scarlet
letter," says Beverly. "It was like I just got out of a cult. I
still have nightmares about him."

Today, Beverly and Johnny are beloved members
of the Chicago and American restaurant community.
(Parachute was nominated as Outstanding Restaurant
in the country at the 2022 James Beard Foundation
Awards.) But there are still vestiges of resentment. In

2021, when I told industry acquaintances in Chicago that Beverly, Johnny, and their team would be the focus of this book, some quietly asked if I knew that she was emotionally delicate.

If I'm honest, I'm conflicted about the lawsuit. On the one hand, Trotter was following what had been normal in his profession for generations. Johnny himself had worked similar jobs early in his career without complaint. On the other, times were changing, as were labor laws. And Trotter was—unlike most fellow toques—independently wealthy, and owned and operated one of the most-high-ticket restaurants in the country; I imagine he could have paid his people for every hour worked without diminishing his own lifestyle.

In any event, life went on, and despite whatever resentments remained among her colleagues, Beverly continued to succeed in a series of jobs. Following her time at Trotter's, she worked for mentor Stegner and George Bumbaris at Prairie Grass Cafe, which they opened in 2004, and for Japanese chef Takashi Yagihashi at his noodle shop at Macy's Chicago. She also made periodic visits to Korea. In 2008, she was named executive chef of Jerry Kleiner's Opera restaurant, where she was working when she received an email and résumé from Johnny Clark, a fellow cook from the Midwest, who had just moved to Chicago following a stint in, of all places, South Korea.

—

Johnny Clark is a native midwesterner, a perennial seeker, and a possessor of demons for many of whom Beverly has been the exorcist.

He was born in September 1970 at The Christ Hospital in Cincinnati, Ohio, the older of two brothers. The son of a graphic designer father and hairdresser mother, he was a gloomy kid, socially awkward, given to cycles of weight gain and loss, and a punching (and kicking) bag for assholes. Acquaintanceships were rare and fleeting until, at thirteen, he discovered skateboarding, which injected his life with exhilaration, a sensation of flight, a mode of transportation to unfamiliar neighborhoods, and connection with fellow lost boys, some of whom he has kept in his orbit into middle age.

Johnny's origin story echoes that of many late twentieth-century American kitchen grunts: antipathy toward traditional classroom education, matriculation at cooking school, and early kitchen jobs in classical French kitchens. But where he's taken his career since those years represents a microcosm of the transition from cooks of the past to a certain type of modern American chef.

Challenged by attention deficit and metastasizing depression, Johnny somnambulated through school, and life. He's unable to decipher now whether the impulse was melodramatic or sincere, but he once fastened a belt around his neck, securing the other end to a shower rod. His feet could reach the floor, but his psychic pain was great enough that he felt compelled to acquaint himself with the noose.

Like so many others before him, Johnny stumbled into his chosen profession: When he turned fifteen, his father insisted he find a job, leading to a dishwashing post at Pelican's Reef, a Key West–inspired canteen up the street from their home, which he recalls as a "Jimmy Buffett–themed place with starfish and shells in epoxy on the tables." In time, he gravitated to the kitchen, at first doing rudimentary tasks, like, say, if service was busy, he'd line red plastic serving baskets with deli paper. He soon found his name on the schedule for cooking shifts during which he'd work the fryer or grill fish, with scant training or expectation; if a fillet left his station with imperfect hashmarks, there wasn't a higher-up or customer who'd notice, or care.

He worked at a series of local restaurants throughout high school, as much for the meager spending money as for the work itself. He quickly demonstrated a natural aptitude, and fascination.

"When I do certain tasks, it feels like that *Matrix* thing for me," he says. "The science of it unfolds, and I get super into it. Like, grilling fish: I know when it's ready to turn, what kind of tool to use for the best effect." The work also busied his mind—a common desire among professional cooks, who also gravitate toward pastimes, like playing a musical instrument, that allow them to lose themselves. "It was kind of like skateboarding, but I was making money," says Johnny.

His father suggested cooking as a career. All Johnny knew was that he wanted to get away from Cincinnati, which for him would forever be haunted by the ghosts of his childhood. And so, after five years in various local restaurant jobs, he matriculated at The Culinary Institute of America (CIA) in Hyde Park, New York, at the time unrivaled as the United States' preeminent professional cooking school.

He started at the CIA in 2000, when old-school tough love endured as a teaching style. No white-coated instructor ever clocked him with a sauté pan, but there was no shortage of table banging, or of their getting in your face and screaming, spraying saliva as if to extinguish your stupidity. He found it degrading, but persevered and thrived. He responded especially well to tactile knowledge, while zoning out on anything book-related.

"That's not why I'm doing this," he remembers thinking of reading assignments. *"I'm doing this to get out of my head."*

He describes his cooking school self as *depressed,* and believes it's what led to his passing obesity. "That, and the milk dispenser [in the cafeteria] and the fact that you could get food all the time."

He and classmate Hung Huynh, a lanky, self-assured Vietnamese American showboater who'd go on to win season 3 of Bravo's *Top Chef*, ventured to Las Vegas together to extern at an outpost of influential American chef Charlie Palmer's seminal New York City restaurant Aureole. I've never eaten at that Aureole, but the thought of Johnny toiling in a Vegas kitchen, in a restaurant remembered for its "wine angels"—sommeliers in harnesses who floated up and down, like Thunderdome competitors, snatching bottles from a massive wine wall—tests the limits of my imagination.

After returning to Hyde Park and completing his culinary studies, Johnny indulged a fascination with history by working at a classic French restaurant in New York City. He trailed at the storied La Caravelle and at the late Sirio Maccioni's celebrity and power magnet Le Cirque, then took a job as a line cook at La Côte Basque, one of the most consequential restaurants in late twentieth-century New York City history, though not mainly for the food. Chef-owner Jean-Jacques Rachou was among the first French-born toques who welcomed young Americans into their ranks in the formative 1980s and '90s. La Côte Basque claims several of the most successful Yanks of that era as alums, including onetime *New York Times* four-star chef David Bouley; the aforementioned New American chef Charlie Palmer; and pastry chef Bill Yosses, who later baked pies for Presidents George W. Bush and Barack Obama as White House pastry chef. By the early 2000s, with New American cuisine well established, and just a beat before the advent of next-wave game changers such as David Chang, La Côte Basque had lapsed into antiquity. But Johnny wasn't chasing the cutting edge; he was more interested in building on the foundation he'd developed at the CIA, cementing French techniques and preparations, and following his own instincts. For a man openly plagued with psychological distress, Johnny's quiet self-belief constantly surprises.

At La Côte Basque, as he had at cooking school, Johnny encountered old-school kitchen brutality. Rachou broke him, he says, by pushing and berating him—*"Move your ass!"*—during service. But you know what they say: *No rain, no flowers.* Johnny developed an emotional callus, a tranquility born of the realization that the worst thing that could happen was that Rachou fire him. He believes that Rachou sensed the shift, and having sensed it, lifted his boot from Johnny's neck.

This will sound like the worst kind of Hollywood sap, but it wasn't long before Johnny developed a love (his word) for Rachou, coming to regard him as a sort-of surrogate grandfather. Rachou's hard-assery was counterbalanced by a soft side, expressed in lavish family (staff) meals prior to service each night, when Rachou set one long table and served a simple, delicious, and civilized meal; a typical fuel-up might include bread, pasta with meat sauce, salad, and cheese. Rachou took a special interest in Johnny. He never voiced sentimentality, but the two of them would plant themselves on milk crates in the chef's office, smoke cigarettes, and shoot the breeze—an atypical dynamic between a culinary lion and one of his cubs. (During one such smoke break, a gourmet organization arrived for a prearranged tour and Rachou, possessed by sudden ennui, pushed a reluctant Johnny into the dining room. "You give them the tour. Tell them you're the chef.") Sometimes, apropos of nothing, Rachou would brush up against Johnny in the kitchen, conspiratorially mutter "Here," and, like a pickpocket operating in reverse, slip him an envelope concealing a stack of hundred-dollar bills—clearly a bonus of some sort, but one which was never discussed or standardized.

Rachou also modeled a life that was rarefied for a chef, and would still be aspirational today. In a pro-

fession known for chewing up even its most successful practitioners, driving them to some combination of
poor health, alcoholism, and/or bankruptcy, Rachou
was as much businessman as culinarian. (Daniel Bou-
lud, the transplanted Lyonnais chef who first came to
New York City in 1982, once told me how impressed he
was when he *staged* for Rachou that year and witnessed
his clever marketing of less expensive cuts of meat
and maximizing of off-cuts in charcuterie—the high-
est expression of phantom frugality.) Decades before
the industry would acknowledge—let alone address—
notions like *balance* and *self-care*, Rachou practiced
them. He also made serious bank at his restaurant and
by investing in New York City real estate.

Despite their personal affinity, over time a chasm
widened between Johnny's nascent culinary sensibility
and Rachou's old-school leanings. Signature dishes,
fussed over and perfected across months and years,
catapulted chefs like Rachou to celebrity, but Johnny
found the repetition stultifying, and the reliance on
out-of-season ingredients to keep those warhorses on
the menu year-round alienated him.

"Some great people came out of that environment,
but I didn't think I'd be able to get to the person I
wanted to be," he says. "*I need to be spontaneous.*"

Not that Johnny equates spontaneity with sloppi-
ness. The menu at Wherewithall changes weekly, but

individual dishes have been altered (sometimes more than once) during their five-day lifespan until the week runs out, or Johnny and Tayler get them sufficiently chiseled, whichever comes first.

"I have these perfectionist qualities," he says. "I have to meet the standards that I have. When I say it doesn't have to be a perfect dish, that's my vision of what cooking is. But when I'm not happy with how a dish comes out, I can't sleep. I have this anxiety until I get it right. I'm sure cooks hated me sometimes because I'll change a dish in the middle of service; we've reprinted menus in the middle of service because I couldn't stand another minute of it."

Anguish tinges his voice as he describes this: not the arrogance of an *artiste*, rather the self-flagellation of a clinical obsessive. During the pandemic he worked on curbing this unforgiving perfectionism, mainly out of consideration for his cooks.

I tell him that this doesn't sound fun, but I relate. I share one of my favorite lines about writing, which I first heard attributed to Ruth Reichl: "I hate writing. I love having written."

He nods affirmatively. "It's pleasurable when I get to that point."

While working in New York City, on the rare occasion he'd dine out—often alone at a restaurant bar—he sometimes encountered signposts pointing him in a stylistic direction. A meal at Greenwich Village's venerable Gotham Bar and Grill—helmed at the time by influential American chef Alfred Portale—loomed large. His meal there comprised tuna tartare and a small roasted sea trout—dishes that struck him as "real," which to him meant free of tricks like the manipulations of modernist techniques and additives that were gaining worldwide traction.

He was also a fan of another, more recently established downtown restaurant, Babbo, led at the time by chef Mario Batali.* It's nothing unusual now, but Babbo's come-as-you-are dress code was envelope-pushing for such a smart, clubby dining space. (The two-story building near Greenwich Village's Washington Square Park had previously housed The Coach House, which opened in the mid-twentieth century and served "continental" cuisine to the *Mad Men* set and their successors for close to half a century.) Babbo's rock-and-roll soundtrack was also brazen; Batali's habit of cranking up the volume when he materialized in the dining room toward closing time in his trademark shorts and orange Crocs was well known throughout the city.

---

* Batali was charged in multiple cases for inappropriate and/or sexually abusive behavior in and out of his restaurants. In one case he was found not guilty. In another he settled with the plaintiff for an undisclosed amount. In 2021, the company he formerly co-operated settled a suit by at least twenty female and male employees who claimed they'd been sexually harassed at three of the company's restaurants, for $600,000. Batali sold his shares in his restaurants in 2019 and now resides in Michigan.

After three years working the fish and appetizer station at La Côte Basque, Johnny moved on to a brief stint at shouty British chef Gordon Ramsay's outpost at The London NYC hotel on the West Side of Manhattan. There he witnessed the most punishing iteration of traditional kitchen sadism he'd yet encountered: Sixteen-hour shifts that dried and cracked fingers and forced tear ducts open—exhausted cooks routinely and spontaneously wept on the line during service. Johnny would stagger back to his Queens apartment around midnight, flop into bed at two A.M.; he refers to the short sleep that followed as "a nap." After a quick shower, he'd pocket a few granola bars—his sole daily sustenance at the time—and catch a subway back to Manhattan. The stint—so brief that he expunged it from future résumés— also strengthened his antipathy to stringent technique and plating, and a lack of improvisation.

"That's when I started to learn what I enjoy doing, and it's spontaneous cooking," he says. "Cooking from the heart and the soul. Sometimes it's not a perfect dish—that's fine. Working with quality products, it's going to be good no matter what, unless I destroy it."

When he reached his physical and emotional break point, he called to tell the restaurant he couldn't take it anymore, missed his shift, and never returned.

Next came Town, a glam, subterranean Geoffrey Zakarian project in midtown Manhattan that preceded the dapper, silver-haired chef's television-fueled second act. A highlight of Johnny's time there was his discovery of Korean food, chowed down on after-hours in Koreatown, the strip of late-night restaurants and karaoke bars on West 32nd Street, their names—many in Korean only—blared loudly in neon and electric, some storefronts squished together so snugly that two or more of them appear to share the same address. Concurrently, he'd read a profile of the Korean chef Im Ji-ho in *Food Arts* magazine, a popular glossy trade publication at the time, with the chef featured on the cover wearing a cap that mimicked a rooster's coxcomb. He was an unconventional chef known for his "aura" cooking—he'd size up a party and improvise their meal, sometimes bolting from the kitchen during service to scavenge for herbs and roots along the nearby mountainside.

In 2008, the old, familiar feeling of being done descended on Johnny again. Done not only with Town, but with New York City. His two gestating interests—Korean food and Chef Im—coalesced into a conviction that he wanted to cook in South Korea, ideally at Chef Im's restaurant Sandang. Trapezing from one job to the next is what aspiring chefs do, but to venture to someplace as distant, culturally and linguistically different, and largely unexplored by American cooks as Korea is, even by today's adventurous standards, extraordinary.

"I'm always the person trying to do something everyone else is not," he says. "Everyone's trying to go to Spain, or maybe even Japan and learn from masters.* I thought, *I want to do something really different. Is there anywhere in Korea I could work?* I didn't know anything about Korea at the time."

An assistant manager at Town called Sandang and spoke to Chef Im on Johnny's behalf, explaining that he'd like to come work for him to learn, and to do it for free. Im wasn't familiar with the Western word *stage*, but told the friend it wasn't the first time he'd been similarly propositioned. He had never felt right about it. This time, though, for unknown reasons, he expressed an openness.

A month later, with no knowledge of the country or the language, Johnny had moved out of his apartment and made his way to Yangpyeong, a small mountain town about thirty miles southeast of Seoul in South Korea's Gyeonggi province. The restaurant was, in Johnny's words, "like a mountain getaway. It was serene, like an oasis. Maybe two-star Michelin [level]." He compares it to the acclaimed Nordic restaurant Noma in that "the food is intricate but natural, trying to mimic nature." Sandang refers to a "house at the foot of a mountain," and that's where it was located,

---

* This was before Scandinavian food had captured the world's imagination.

facilitating foraging and cooking with freshly plucked ingredients.

Beyond the cuisine and ambience, Johnny was also taken with the fact that "[Im] was an artist," who'd use paper, paint, and markers to create a spontaneous work for everyone who dined there. "More than fifty people [a night]," says Johnny. "He did an aura painting for everyone. It was unbelievable."

Johnny was the only Westerner on staff and the only one whose first language was English. The job wasn't cushy: He and his co-workers lived in converted construction trailers, two people to a room, and slept on roll-up mats on the heated floor; in the morning, you walked outside in a robe and flip-flops and showered in one of the gender-specific communal washrooms.

Per house policy, he started as a busboy, the philosophy being that regardless of prior experience, one was expected to work their way into this specific kitchen.

On paper, the schedule was as taxing as those of the Western restaurants where he'd trained in New York City. Here he worked six days a week, both lunch and dinner, meaning he arrived around seven A.M., the air misty, the grass slickened with dew, and didn't return to his trailer until around ten P.M. But the culture was much kinder. "It was the first time where I worked in a kitchen where no one was rude," he says. "There was no competitiveness. Nobody was trying to get ahead of you. There was no need for that. There was no loud talking, no screaming. Everyone was working in peace and working great."

Further, the commute was a short stroll, and Im fed his people three square meals a day, arrayed on tables, banquet style. Im also surprised Johnny by paying him, in cash, starting his first week. "I left with more money than I came with," says a still-disbelieving Johnny today.

Im spoke scant English, but Johnny found it easy to communicate with him wordlessly, through panto-mime, exaggerated facial expressions, and carefully calibrated grunts and murmurs.

"I know it sounds like a fairy tale," Johnny says. "But that's just how it was."

Do you believe in fate? If you don't, then Johnny Clark must be the luckiest guy on planet Earth. How did this shy, lanky, picked-on, given-to-depression cook land in not one but *two* professional kitchens run by soulmates? I mention to him that Rachou was an or-phan whose childhood in adopted homes was so brutal and (it is believed by many who know him) abusive that for decades he has declined to discuss it in inter-views. In response, Johnny shares with me that Im, too, had had a tumultuous childhood: He ran away from home in his teens, lived on the streets for a spell, then found work making fine charcoal—an art in Korea and Japan. Among his tasks was delivering charcoal to businesses, including restaurants, where he'd enter via the back door right into the kitchen, a setting which intrigued him.

"These are pretty big coincidences," I observe. "You falling under the wing of these two guys."

"I don't know," Johnny says, shaking his head. This may be a good time to mention that Johnny is soft spoken. He has the energy, disposition, and fashion sense of a prototypical evolved Bay Area or Pacific Northwest dude—calm, gentle, patient, with facial hair that's apt to change length and configuration between sightings. In conversation, he might display frustration or, more likely, bewilderment with something vexing, but almost never anger.

"Maybe there is some coincidence there. I never thought about it. Up to this point those were the two most influential people in my career. I really do believe that people are attracted to each other by their likenesses. Maybe it was something from my childhood, being picked on, but I never felt comfortable in groups. I still don't feel comfortable in groups or clubs. [Im and Rachou] were doing their own thing. Even Rachou wasn't focused on other chefs."

As with Rachou, Johnny also was drawn to Im's balanced life. "I enjoy the chefs who are not just working but into *life*, and working as part of life. I took that away." He also found hope in the style of kitchen leadership, that "there doesn't need to be some full on anger/ego situation; you can cook for happiness."

His time in Korea as the lone Caucasian also granted Johnny new and valuable perspective: "I won't say I understand what it's like to be a minority in [the United States]," he says. "But for the first time I understood what it's like to be 'the other.' I was completely ignorant before that. I grew up in Ohio. Even in New York, I was just working. I never thought of other people's feelings as minorities; it wasn't even on my radar. I always felt like I was not prejudiced, but this wasn't a thing I thought about."

Eventually at Sandang he was allowed to help with some prep, like making industrial-sized batches of kimchi or wrapping fish; observe other tasks; and plate cold salads during service. By then, three months had passed; it was time to renew his visa or risk deportation. By month four, unable to extend his credentials, Johnny returned to the States. If not for the legal hurdle, he might have stayed at Sandang for years, but wasn't willing to risk a lifetime expulsion. Instead, he arrived back in New York, so broke he couldn't afford a storage facility, let alone rent. He shipped his possessions to Chicago, where he crashed in his brother's apartment for a few months, sleeping—as he'd done in Yangpyeong—on the floor. He and Im independently tried to secure a work visa that would enable Johnny to return. (There being no shortage of cooks in Korea, the visa was repeatedly denied on the basis that Johnny would be taking a job from a national.)

Finally, one of Im's assistants called Johnny to explain that the chef was moving on.

More dominoes toppled. The economy crashed in fall 2008, restaurants suffered, and jobs vanished. He *staged* for an ambitious tasting-menu restaurant, but found it anxiety provoking and claustrophobic, and quit after one night.

"I don't even know why I tried," says Johnny. "I know I don't want to do that. But something about the culinary culture in this country says that's what you need to do if you want to be a 'real' chef.

"I get the camaraderie thing and the ability to use it on your résumé," he says. "But that's not going to make *me* happy. I just from the bottom of my heart love cooking. Cooking for people. That's what makes me happy. That keeps me out of my depression. I think of it like cooking for somebody in my home. 'I have these products; why don't you come over for dinner?' I'm trying to *not* show off. There's nothing to prove. But in a [Michelin] three-star [restaurant], these dishes are probably rehearsed for months before they go on the menu. I just feel like there's a lot more at stake when you're charging people eight hundred dollars for dinner."

Johnny helps Thomas hone his butchery skills.

—

As much as any other consideration, money drives
fledgling cooks' decision making. Save it up and you
can take time off, regroup between jobs, maybe travel.
But run out, and it's back to the grind. Johnny had run
out. Chicago had already begun its march toward its
current exalted place in the restaurant ecosystem—
classics like Charlie Trotter's were still in operation,
and Grant Achatz's modernist Alinea had debuted in
2005. But Johnny wanted to continue his exploration
of Korean cuisine, "to hold onto a piece of that," and the
city was essentially bereft of Korean restaurants save
for mom-and-pop places where Johnny didn't want to

work and, as a White man and non-family member, likely wouldn't have been hired anyway.

Around this time, flipping through an issue of *CS* magazine, a local luxury-lifestyle publication, he stuck on a feature article profiling some local chefs, including Beverly Kim, then working at Opera. His curiosity piqued by her Korean heritage, he dug a little further online, and discovered a video of Beverly uncharacteristically vamping, emerging from between two curtains to purr, "Welcome to Opera."

He was intrigued.

"I felt like I came away from Korea with a new wholesomeness in my life and I thought, this is a person I want to know," he says. "She seemed super fun. That's the way I wish I could be on camera—charismatic and funny and witty."

Beverly had only recently been promoted to executive chef. She thinks the *CS* profile was her print-media debut. At the time of the shoot, she had worked thirty days straight, without a sous chef. So she showed up with frizzled hair and a wrinkled chef's jacket, and when the time came for her close-up, struck an awkward pose.

"That was the picture he saw," she laughs. Of the video that attracted him, she says, "I was a little loopy."

The résumé Johnny sent was as minimalist as the yet-to-be-conceived Wherewithall's menu: restaurants worked, positions held, dates of service. There was no embellishing text, no lofty "objective." The document was an elegant counterpoint to the puffery of many young cooks' résumés, and it froze Beverly, as did the time spent at Sandang. She remembered the *Food Arts* cover story about Im, in whites and a rooster cap, his foraging for unheralded ingredients, his shamanistic credentials. Had she known about him sooner, she would have tried to work for him herself. By the time she was done daydreaming about who might have composed this résumé, she had conjured an image of a fascinating cook who'd had the foresight to apprentice in Korea before its cuisine penetrated the mainstream American dining consciousness as it has in recent years. She also, it must be said, thought that "Johnny Clark" was Black.

A rendezvous was set. Beverly and Johnny met after service one night at Wabash Tap, a watering hole down the block from Opera. Per their emails, they brought along pictures of their Korean adventures so they could compare notes. Before they got to that, Beverly was struck by a tattoo just below Johnny's right wrist—three little hibiscuses meant to be the *mugunghwa*, Korea's national flower. Impressed, she asked him what his favorite Korean food was. This was a test. Bibimbap or bulgogi would have been too normal, banal, and a nonstarter. Instead, his flying-colors answer was *chung gook jang*, a fermented soy bean soup, so foul-smelling that it's left off the roster even in many Korean restaurants.

Johnny had come to love it as a perpetually hungry cook in Im's kitchen, where it was sometimes served for staff meal. It happens to be one of Beverly's favorite foods, soulful and ugly-delicious (the phrase coined by Korean American superstar chef David Chang as an Instagram hashtag to describe visually sketchy food that tastes awesome).

"It was like fireworks from the beginning," says Beverly. Within a month, they were engaged in a courtship, though the budding relationship remained chaste; to pursue it honestly, they both broke up with their respective significant others. Beverly moved in with her sister. "Every day was like romance. It was more like I felt like I met my soulmate," remembers Beverly. "So many things we shared and talked about. So much in common but also so different." They also, almost immediately, began thinking about a Korean restaurant they might open together someday.

That restaurant, Parachute, became a reality and a success six years later. The intervening time, however, tested them more than anything they had endured individually. Johnny foundered professionally, never finding his professional place in Chicago. A low point came when he cooked an audition menu for the executive chef position at C-House, a Marcus Samuelsson restaurant. He thought he'd nailed it and gotten the job, but instead was offered a sous chef position. Seeking sufficient stability to start a family, he left the restaurant world altogether and took a job at Whole Foods on North Halsted Street in Chicago's Lakeview neighborhood. Beverly, increasingly frustrated by the conflict between the stages of her personal life (wanting to have children) and career (moving up to positions that required more time), soon followed. And just like that, these two industrious culinarians with enviable credentials were laboring as hot-bar cooks, dumping bins of mac and cheese into steam tables. If there were portals *out* of the industry, this was surely one of them.

"We felt like our dreams were slipping away," says Beverly. "That's what killed us the most."

Desperate for an emotional life raft, Beverly fell under the spell of *The Secret*, the spiritual bestselling book, video, and cultural phenomenon that promised that if you wished for and believed in something strongly enough, it would come true. It sounds as silly as a Pet Rock now, but many bought into it at the time, including Oprah Winfrey, who devoted two episodes of her popular talk show to it.

"Much of that concept is kind of goofy, but I do think there's a truth in keeping your vision present in your mind every day," says Johnny.

Adds Beverly: "It helped us determine what we value together. We value family. We value excellence. We value adventure. We value acknowledgment because we believe that acknowledgment will get you business and we wanted our own restaurant."

Following the book's advice, Beverly and Johnny fashioned a vision board with pictures representing their goals, such as a photograph of a family.

"It was a fun exercise," says Beverly. "It made us smile putting it together. After we did that vision board, I got pregnant. We had a shotgun wedding after six months." On the inside of both their wedding rings, they had the same message inscribed: JAMES BEARD, TOP CHEF, GOURMET MAGAZINE, even though they had nothing to their name. Like so many of their colleagues, for all they'd accomplished they were still employees, renters, dreamers.

Following the birth of their first son, Daewon, in January 2010, the couple remained dissatisfied creatively, but appreciated the finite nature of the work. "When you're done, you're done," says Beverly. "You don't take any of it home."

Still, their schedule was taxing, and isolating: Beverly would leave their home at five A.M. and walk to Whole Foods, arriving at six. She'd work an eight-hour shift, then Johnny would hand Daewon off to her as he was headed into his two P.M. to ten P.M. shift. This eliminated the expense of childcare, though they racked up substantial medical bills resulting from health care premiums and co-pays.

"We were paying $500 per month for my maternity," says Beverly. "We were considering other careers." She pondered returning to school. Johnny thought about construction, and applied for a job with UPS.

Instead, they ended up in Ohio, helping out Johnny's father with Lucky John Slow Market, a gourmet grocery he'd opened a few years earlier, after losing his graphic design job in the 2008 recession. Johnny worked with his father and Beverly transferred to a local Whole Foods. There surely were other Asian people in Cincinnati at the time, but Beverly never crossed paths with them, which deepened her sense of isolation. At work, she was passed over for a promotion that went to, in her estimation, a less qualified White man. Merging into traffic one day, a White driver harassed them, all but running their car off the road, lowering his window to cackle, "Go home, you Jap!" at Beverly.

"I didn't even know what I was feeling," says Beverly. "I felt like I was going back in time. I just felt . . . *different*."

When she got off work at two P.M., Beverly would beeline for Lucky John to help clean. But for all their efforts, the business failed.

Beverly Kim and Tayler Ploshehanski confer in the Wherewithall kitchen.

"It wasn't set up for success," says Johnny. "I feel like if we did the same concept on Logan Square [in Chicago] it would have been successful."

"So now we're in Cincinnati," says Beverly. "I felt a withering away of my dreams personally."

"I felt the same," says Johnny. "I moved down here to try to make something of the place. . . . I killed myself trying."

Just in time, a deus ex machina: A recruiter contacted Beverly, asking her to audition for a chef position at the Chicago restaurant Aria that required some fluency in Asian cuisine. She worked her way up the hierarchy over the course of five telephone interviews, finally talking with the general manager. She was flown to Chicago to prepare four dishes for an audition menu. She was fearful, out of the game so long that she wondered how rusty she'd become and if she'd embarrass herself. For his part, Johnny wondered if she wanted to go back to the big city, reassume all that stress.

After almost a year in Cincinnati limbo, when finally offered the job, Beverly's answer was swift: "Yes!" They moved back to Chicago and Beverly started at Aria in February 2011.

It was about this time that *Top Chef* came into their lives. Beverly auditioned for and was chosen as a *cheftestant* for the show's ninth season. They'd flipped the script from unbearable despair to a surfeit of opportunity. Overwhelmed, they turned the vision board around to stymie its power.

"I don't think that it worked," clarifies Johnny. "We *made* it work by having this vision in our head every day. And ninety percent of that vision board happened. It was about keeping the goals. I think there's so many moments in the day, you wake up, and it's 'Ah, shit, I need to go to work. I fucking hate this traffic.' You don't think about your goals at all, and the days go by."

Top Chef season 9 filmed in mid-2011 and started airing that November. The season features series mainstays Tom Colicchio, Gail Simmons, Hugh Acheson,

Emeril Lagasse, and Padma Lakshmi, with the by-now-familiar rewards on the line for the winner: a feature in *Food & Wine* magazine, a showcase at the Food & Wine Classic at Aspen, and $125,000 to help bring their culinary dream to life.

Set in Texas, the season features all the hallmarks of the long-running series: The *cheftestants* visit key cities such as Dallas, and landmarks such as The Alamo in San Antonio. They improvise dishes with culinary totems of the setting: rattlesnake, short ribs, and chiles. They incorporate placed products, whether matching food to Don Julio tequila or driving to Whole Foods in Toyota Siennas. And they cook for a murderer's row of guest judges including Michelin three-star chef Eric Ripert; Los Angeles's Mary Sue Milliken and Susan Feniger; and—incongruously—diva Patti LaBelle and Oscar-winning actress Charlize Theron.

In the center of the storm is a thirty-two-year-old, bewildered Beverly Kim, going by Beverly Kim *Clark* in early episodes, enrobed in a black chef's coat with Aria emblazoned on the left breast.

Eight years after polarizing the Chicago restaurant community with the Trotter lawsuit, Beverly divides the *Top Chef* competitor pool. On the show, she comes off as a quirky open book: Still in the grip of *The Secret*, she keeps a folded note in her pocket that reads I can. I must. I will. She tapes a handwritten sign on her

shared bedroom window that says, CONGRATULATIONS
TOP CHEF BEVERLY KIM. In the confessional and other
interviews, she speaks about having a husband and son
back in Chicago, having to bring home the bacon, and
that "if I believe it, I can achieve it."

She also fumbles through a few klutzy moments—
spraying co-host Padma Lakshmi and modernist cuisine guru Nathan Myhrvold with an ISI gun,* and
setting off a smoke detector. And she commits a cardi-
nal kitchen sin, usually performed in shameful solitude
in the walk-in: While awaiting the results of a rodeo-
themed cooking challenge, she *cries* over how much
she misses Johnny.

Ironically, Nyesha Arrington, a Black female
California-based chef who, like Beverly, is of (partial)
Korean descent and came up in old-school French
kitchens, is among her most vocal critics on the show:
"There's no crying in cooking. On a personal level,
I'm a very compassionate person but you can't let
your emotions show with the rest of the group or
they'll perceive you as weak."

Counterbalancing Nyesha's sentiments are those
of Edward Lee, a Korean American chef, restaurateur,
and author (his *Buttermilk Graffiti* is essential reading)

---

* an aerator for making foams, and one of the most used devices in modernist
cuisine

who since his *Top Chef* stint has become a sainted figure in the industry for his LEE Initiative, which supports a variety of local and national causes. Before the season's over he comments that he respects Beverly as a person and chef.

In hindsight, the season presents as a microcosm of industry dysfunction: In the fourth episode, Richie Farina, a sous chef at Moto, is sent home. "I didn't show what Moto can do," he sobs to a fellow cook from the restaurant, in an accidental near-parody of chef personality cults. Episode 5 features as guest judge John Besh, the New Orleans chef and restaurateur who was the first chef-predator uncovered in what became known as the #MeToo movement. And season winner Paul Qui was subsequently revealed to be a domestic abuser.

Unlike, say, *Survivor*, on which competitors vote each other off, *Top Chef* always comes down to the cooking and the judges' evaluation of it. And Beverly has cooking chops, more than most of her competitors. When the time comes to represent, more often than not she does: She whips up an octopus dish based on *nakji bokkeum*, a Korean classic her mom used to make featuring grilled scallions and pickled cucumbers; a rattlesnake nigiri with Thai basil–jalapeño aioli; short ribs with kimchi; and a chile-crusted tuna with habanero-pineapple salsa; and she is announced the winner of the season's "Restaurant

War" episode—a favorite among industry viewers—for her braised short rib dish, earning her a trip to Napa Valley and a bottle of wine I won't name; they didn't pay *me* for the product placement.

After surviving nine episodes, Beverly is voted out by the judges on episode 10—they didn't dislike her dish, it's just that at that point in the competition, even a good one can get you sent home. She returns in episode 14 as the victor of "Last Chance Kitchen," a running competition among losers, but her return proves short-lived.

Her *Top Chef* adventure accelerated Beverly's personal and professional development and maturation. She regards it as one of the most risky, challenging things she's attempted, and is proud of her showing. The constant pressure to create spontaneously and in isolation, without a team or chef-husband off whom to bounce ideas, strengthened her confidence in her talent and culinary "voice." And the extended time away from her family to help advance a long-term goal granted her greater mental and emotional stamina. She didn't come away a victor, but she had no regrets. (Her appearance on the show was also what got her parents to finally stop pressuring her to go back to school and switch careers.)

—

Top Chef **marked** a reversal of fortune for Beverly, and the family overall. But for Johnny, things had stagnated. As Beverly continued to work, he stayed home taking care of Daewon, busying himself when possible with handiwork to occupy his mind. But it wasn't possible often with his parental responsibilities.

"It was very hard," he says. "I don't do well alone without someone to talk to. I feel like I'm a pretty good dad. There wasn't enough handiwork for me to do. Anything I *could* find, like fixing the house, building a piece of furniture, you can't do while watching a kid. I couldn't find anything to satisfy that need to soothe that anxiety. Beverly and I looked at each other one day and thought, *Is this it for us?* Somebody's going to work, somebody's going to stay home?"

For such a modest guy, Johnny possesses a strong sense of destiny. He was convinced that staying at home would break him, set off a psychic chain reaction from which he might never recover.

"I'm not going to be a good person after a few years," he remembers thinking. Existential doubt seeped into his thinking as he questioned his value to himself and his family.

"I couldn't see that I'm a dad. I *do* have a lot of purpose," he says. "For me it was like a deep empty hole inside. Then, in turn, I felt like I wasn't being a good dad. *Then* felt guilty that I wasn't raising him properly.

Then it felt like *oh fuck being on this planet. I don't know what I'm doing anymore.*"

I tell Johnny about a late-breaking depression I experienced, that peaked when I was about thirty. One spectacular spring Sunday, when we lived together in Manhattan's Chelsea neighborhood, my girlfriend at the time (now wife) returned home after lunch with friends to find me still in my night clothes, sitting on our living room sofa, the blinds drawn, the room dark and silent.

"I've been there," he says. "I would just lay in bed. I would stick my kid in front of a screen. I just couldn't feel anything anymore."

Johnny had seen therapists on and off his whole life, and at Beverly's insistence, he started again around this time.

It was also around this time when, unexpectedly, came the spark that in time would inspire Wherewithall: Johnny began reading about the neo-bistro movement in France—places that were shrugging off the approval of the *Guide Michelin* in favor of simple food served in a convivial environment. In January 2012, David Chang wrote a *New York Times* piece titled "Where to Go Eat in 2012," sharing favorite bites from his global travels. In it, he wrote lovingly of Le Châteaubriand on Avenue Parmentier in Paris's Eleventh Arrondissement. "The chef is Iñaki Aizpitarte—there's nobody like him," enthused Chang. "He's doing food in new ways, and in the sort of relaxed setting that you might find in America but is rare in Paris."

The more Johnny learned about Le Châteaubriand and its quietly inventive dishes, the more strongly he sensed a kindred spirit behind it, and an outline of the personal culinary style toward which he'd been struggling.

"It looked like what I had been trying to achieve in my head but couldn't quite do," he says.

Through a former La Côte Basque colleague, he connected with Laurent Cabut, one of Le Châteaubriand's owners, who invited him to *stage*, but not for just a week, as Johnny had envisioned; instead, the restaurant insisted that *stagiaires* work a month. Beverly consented and Johnny's father helped by caring for Daewon. Johnny's friend Quentin, living in Paris at the time, invited him to sleep on his pull-out couch for a month, and fed Johnny during his stay. Had any of those tumblers not fallen into place, it wouldn't have been possible. "We were so broke. People were super generous," says Johnny, including the team at Le Châteaubriand, where he worked for free. "They were generous in letting me come," he says. "It was a tiny kitchen; there really wasn't room for me there."

On-the-ground reality matched media hype, and Le Châteaubriand reinvigorated Johnny. "It wasn't the El

Bulli kind of experimentation," he says. "It was natural food, natural ingredients, presented in a way I'd never seen before. It was super eye-opening, another springboard in my career that I could tie into my experience that shaped me in one month." (It's also where Johnny picked up the inspiration for Wherewithall's unusual expediting sheets.)

Johnny didn't get to know Inaki well, but it's worth noting that the Basque-born chef was, like Rachou and Im before him, something of a soulmate: a wanderer who had been a stone carver and landscape painter before landing in Tel Aviv and taking a job as a dishwasher in, of all places, a Serbian restaurant. After multiple relocations and kitchen positions, he arrived back in Paris, where he drew attention at a series of experimental venues before taking the helm at Le Châteaubriand.

Coincidentally, I was in Paris on a working trip in October 2021, and made a point of dining at Le Châteaubriand. The impact on Johnny and Wherewithall isn't telegraphed by the decor; the space that houses Le Châteaubriand dates back to the 1930s and has preserved many original design elements. Moreover, the kitchen isn't open; the bar is in the dining room, not a separate space; and guests aren't presented with a printed menu, which changes daily—not weekly like Wherewithall's—and is conveyed by servers verbally in each party's choice of French or English. But as soon as dishes started materializing, the influence was obvious. There's an optional wine pairing (we ordered it). A few snacks appeared—gougères followed by a beguiling shot of what the server calls "liquid ceviche," tinged red by the onions within, made by straining a traditional ceviche.* A basket of warm bread arrived. Plated dishes were elemental but refined: The fish course was a morsel of red mullet, a cube of cooked pumpkin, and a tiny quenelle of minced ginger, arranged at two, six, and ten o'clock on the plate. The meat was venison, served bathed in a chestnut-hued sauce fashioned from its stock, and a sheepshead mushroom most accurately described as *phallic* alongside. We were offered cheese *or* dessert. (Deepening the similarities between Le Châteaubriand and Wherewithall: Today Le Châteaubriand has a sister restaurant, Le Dauphin, by the same owners, a few doors down the street.)

We had a 9:30 P.M. table, late even by mid-COVID Paris standards, so were the last guests to leave. As they completed their tasks, the staff gathered at a cluster of tables near the street side of the restaurant, drink-

---

* It's not as clever as it may sound. This is *leche de tigre* ("tiger's milk"), a popular drink in its native Peru.

ing wine, laughing, unwinding. I think of the team at Wherewithall doing the same. Neither restaurant started this tradition, but it's a reminder of the shared industry rituals that transcend generations, geographical boundaries, and languages.

Johnny says that Im Ji-ho had the greatest impact on his *life*, but that Iñaki Aizpitarte was his culinary North Star.

Later that year, Beverly and Johnny were jointly hired as chef of Bonsoirée, a Chicago restaurant that had recently earned a Michelin star. They took the job, but their Korean-inspired menu failed to gain traction and they left after three months. On top of that, once they began working there in earnest, it quickly became apparent to them that the restaurant was headed inexorably toward permanent closure. (It did indeed shut down after their departure.) It was a fraught context in which to test their ability to collaborate, but they recognized that as a product of circumstance and didn't let it deter them from their plans. For the time being, though, it was back to one-off gigs when they could get them, until Johnny took an hourly position at Prairie Grass Cafe and Beverly accepted the teaching position at Kendall. But even that was postponed due to lack of matriculation for the summer module.

Finally, they arrived at a shared epiphany: It was time to open their own restaurant and let its success or failure determine their future. They wrote a business plan for what would become Parachute, centered on a $250,000 investment, roughly half the national average for a comparable restaurant at the time. They borrowed $110,000 from Beverly's parents, which was essentially the money they had planned to spend on college, and then on her wedding. "I convinced them to reinvest in me," says Beverly, who considers the moment her parents' "redemption" for not believing in and supporting her career from the get-go. She and Johnny supplemented that with a $120,000 bank loan, and a friend gifted them $6,000.

It took a full year to find the right home for the concept. Finally, in September 2013 they found a fifteen-hundred-square-foot space on North Elston Avenue in Avondale, then operating as Dos Sabores (Two Flavors), a taqueria and Mexican bakery, and signed a lease that went into effect on November 1, 2013.

During the build-out, Johnny worked at chef Jason Hammel's nearby Lula Cafe from four A.M. to one P.M., then went to Parachute. He sometimes spontaneously passed out. His knees suffered for his overexertion, so much so that for a brief time he had to use a cane.

Their business plan was tight: They were to take a

combined salary of $35,000 in year one. (Some colleagues advised them to not take any.)

By the opening in May 2014, son Daewon was four. They lived below the poverty line, qualifying Daewon for free preschool under the Head Start program.

Fortunately, the restaurant was a success. *Chicago Tribune* critic Phil Vettel enthused that, "For my money... Parachute is the most exciting restaurant to open in Chicago this year." Michelin bestowed a star. *Bon Appétit* included Parachute on its annual rundown of the nation's best new restaurants. And Beverly and Johnny jointly received the James Beard Foundation Award as Best Chef, Great Lakes.

The restaurant enjoyed a terrific run and five years later, in 2019, Beverly and Johnny launched Wherewithall just down the street, in a building they also purchased. Initially Wherewithall hewed even closer to the Le Châteaubriand model, with a daily changing four-course menu served in the dining room. Like Parachute before it, Wherewithall was warmly received. Eight months later, the pandemic shut it all down.

Following her graduating Kendall, Tayler returned to Blackbird for a year and a half, and she and Beverly lost touch, except for the occasional encounter at events and the Green City Market.

There are factors in a cook's life that influence decisions in ways civilians might never consider: Tayler
requested lunch shifts, but not because she was a
morning person or had a special affinity for soups and
salads. Rather, she lived in West Humboldt Park, a desolate neighborhood requiring a multi-bus odyssey com-
mencing after service, which in the evening could be as
late as midnight. In major metropolises, few are the line
cooks whose commute clocks in at less than an hour and
doesn't present at least one dicey train line or city block.

In time, she did move on to dinner, eventually working every station. It was an ongoing test: Even *garmo*, the
starting-level position in many kitchens, was unusually
challenging, with two cooks executing ten dishes. Among
those that lodge in her memory: halibut with shaved radishes, freekeh, little "lime Doritos" (lime *suprêmes* cut into
tiny triangles), pickled mustard seeds, mustard "broth"
(like a broken vinaigrette with mustard seed oil and lime
leaf) and mustard greens; grilled sturgeon with fingerling
potatoes, roasted leeks, and ham hock broth; sweetbreads
with wax beans, hazelnut cream, and hazelnut crumble;
and lamb tartare.

In contrast to many aspiring chefs, especially big-city
ones, Tayler didn't devote her off-hours to an obsessional
quest for culinary knowledge and inspiration. Oh, she
might watch chef-centered shows like Netflix's hagiog-
raphic series *Chef's Table*, but she wasn't on a mission,

and wasn't into cookbooks until assuming her position at Wherewithall and seeking inspiration and new techniques. (The week I observed, she based the tart on a recipe in Francisco Migoya's book *The Elements of Dessert*.) She enjoyed making pasta and playing around at home, hitting on new combinations and ideas through trial and error.

In time, she moved up the line, eventually becoming David Posey's sous chef.

Tayler considers herself a proactive manager, owing to Posey's orientation.

"One thing David really taught us is that you have to assume everything is wrong. As his sous chef for four years, I'm always looking at things and thinking, *Is it wrong? How is it wrong? How can I fix it as quickly as possible?*"

Then it was onto Publican's pastry department under Anna Posey, David's wife, to develop basic dessert-making techniques, then to Intro, a Chicago restaurant that booked a roster of visiting chefs, to which she was attracted for the possibility of working under various talents for a few months each, without having to acclimate to a new environment.

She killed time for a year at avec under Perry Hendrix while David Posey was readying his restaurant Elske for its launch, then moved there to be his opening sous chef in 2016. She remained in that position until the pandemic closed the restaurant indefinitely in 2020. (It reopened in December 2021.) That's about when Beverly reached out to her about joining the team at Wherewithall, initially working in the community kitchen they ran during the first months of the pandemic. Over time, Tayler was charged with running the canteen, leading to four days of work per week, which was a practical and emotional relief. (Cooks rarely know what to do with a life deprived of kitchen time and structure.) When the pandemic began, in fits and starts, to lift in 2021, other restaurants approached Tayler about joining them, but she went with the Wherewithall position.

To see Tayler going about her business at Wherewithall, matter-of-factly correcting her charges on the fine points of butchery, plating, and time management, you'd never guess at her youthful insecurities. At the same time, she's something of a stealth leader. During a follow-up conversation at the end of the week I spent at the restaurant, I confessed that on day one (Tuesday), I had no idea how she spent most of her time between the menu meeting and the commencement of service. Turns out she had floated, helping whoever might need a hand with prep, calling vendors to check on errant deliveries, answering cooks' questions, interviewing prospective employees in the restaurant's sun-flooded dining room, and participating in manager-level meetings. You know that picture of the White House Situation Room during the raid on the Pakistani compound that resulted in the capture and killing of Osama Bin Laden? The one where President Obama is sitting among the cabinet members and multistar military figures, in command but laying back as others execute? That's what I think of when I consider Tayler's management style.

For the moment, she's eyeing a round of meat courses—not bound for Table 12, but nearing completion for a different deuce and a four-top. Reuben sets tomatoes down on a half-dozen plates, Thomas spoons sauce over them. In the dish, the influences of Johnny, Beverly, and Tayler herself are no longer distinguishable from one another. It is a product of their individual pasts and shared present, their brainstorms and sudden bursts of inspiration, trial and error, necessity and invention. Its flavors and textures testify to the practices of the farms they support and the teachings that their chefs imparted to them and that they've imparted to the cooks. It is a summation of their lives, the week, and the day. Of course, the guests cannot discern all of that, and it doesn't matter. It's all there, in every bite. Whether they know it or not, it's all there.

6

Plate-Up

In Wherewithall's basement, at the foot of a steep and narrow stairway, stands one of the unseen heroes of Wherewithall's operation: Blanca Vasquez. A resettled Ecuadorian who amassed a lifetime of physical fortitude as a child laborer harvesting sugarcane and rice in the fields of Cuenca, Blanca has never dined at the restaurant upstairs, and speaks only Spanish. She cleans what remains of strangers' meals from plates and bowls, glasses and silverware, blasting them with an industrial sink sprayer, augmenting its force with her own, scrubbing with sponges and steel wool to erase any stubborn streaks and stuck-on bits.

At forty-nine, Blanca, Wherewithall's dishwasher, is solidly built, with tan skin, and stands upright in her kitchen clogs. As much as the cooks, she has a signature kitchen getup: hair pulled back in a bun and framed by

Blanca Vasquez, dialed in during the heat of service

a purple fabric headband festooned above the forehead with a facsimile of a flower fashioned from the same cloth. The band, tilted downward toward the back, pins her glasses' temples firmly in place where they disappear behind her ears. She wears a loose-fitting blouse striped with primary colors, guarded from spatter by a thin white apron loosely tied so it leans out in front of her, like a drawbridge.

Blanca's hometown of Cuenca is situated in northern Ecuador. The oldest of nine siblings, she's been doing physical work since age nine, when her mother sat her down and told her that, once she herself died, it would fall to Blanca to support her brother and seven sisters. (Her mother survives to this day, but has buried five of Blanca's siblings.)

When she was just eleven, Blanca paired up with the man who would father her children. "It's a hard life," her mother told her. "That's what you do."

By the time the man abandoned her, they had three daughters. In 2004, at age thirty-two, in order to earn money to send home, Blanca emigrated to the United States, leaving her children behind. (She tells me this and the rest of her story in Spanish at Wherewithall in the hour before service, as José Villalobos translates for us.) The group with whom she traveled chose Chicago, and so she found herself there by default. That time conjures a mishmash of conflicting emotions: abiding sorrow at not seeing her daughters for years, nostalgia for playing like a child in the snow at the onset of her first midwestern American winter.

Blanca possesses a vague sense of the Wherewithall dining experience—that there are courses devoted to fish, meat, and so on. She recognizes that it's an entirely different style of food and service from the nondescript joints, the names of which she's long since forgotten, where she worked previously. At home, Blanca delights in cooking, preparing Ecuadorian meatballs, fried fish, fish stew, mariscos (shellfish), chicken, and beans—especially white and canary—for friends. In recent years, she's scaled back, only expending the time and energy when large groups gather for festivals or holidays. She's skilled enough that, in Ecuador, she worked for a time in restaurants that served traditional dishes, as what she calls "the cook," meaning the chef. This explains something that happens during our conversation: As she describes the food she likes to make, she exhibits a telltale habit of professional cooks, mimicking the repetitive movements grooved into muscle memory. Her hands dance over and around each other, miming their machinations in each dish's preparation—the hands flip imaginary fish, toss shrimp in a phantom hot pan, and shake an unseen pot of beans. Perhaps it's but a dream, but if presented with a chance to cook professionally again, or somehow to own a restaurant, she'd take it.

Immigration brought a demotion, from cook to dishwasher. When her most recent employer had to let her go, the informal network of local kitchen workers directed her to Parachute, where she was hired, and then transferred to sister restaurant Wherewithall.

For a restaurant worker, Blanca's shifts are unusually isolated: She doesn't speak English, and so her interaction with most of the staff is limited to the kitchen crew's hollers of "hola, hola" that greet her when she rolls in about an hour before service each night and disappears down the stairs. A few employees, like José, speak Spanish and periodically check in on her. She wishes she could understand everyone, or even just make small talk. And most of her hours are passed in the basement, only seeing her co-workers when they breeze past to fetch something from the walk-in or dry storage area.

Given her limited knowledge of kitchen and dining room protocols, Blanca's keeping them well equipped depends on evidentiary clues such as what arrives in the tubs that Hector Blacio, the restaurant's polisher—and not incidentally one of her sons-in-law—shuttles down to her. Mixed in with serveware and silverware are equipment: pots and pans, spoons and strainers, whisks and mixing bowls, and any other utensil or vessel that might have been sullied by diner or cook. All of it must be returned to the speedway as soon as possible, so Blanca's priorities shift by the minute. Generally, especially early in the night, she cleans a little of everything in each batch Hector deposits on the stainless-steel receiving shelf, resembling a solitaire player as she arranges and rearranges them in a poly-propylene peg rack to maximize its confines. Once it's at capacity, she slides the rack into the warewasher (the machine that blasts them clean with scalding hot water) and activates it. Minutes later, she lifts the cover, and the items reemerge through a burst of steam, reborn in the sanitizing heat.

As the hours tick by, especially on Saturday night, instinct drives Blanca to clean ever faster. If a pileup of dirty dishes and equipment gathers, she's going too slowly. If she discerns an especially large number of, say, dinner plates, she'll prioritize those—if there are twenty, she'll do ten, along with a hodgepodge of other items, then do the remaining ten in the next batch, and so on.

In addition to Hector, Blanca is aided in her work by Manuel Astimbay, lean and muscular, her domestic partner and weekend backup. As he will be most of the night, Manuel is stationed behind her, and swiftly towel-dries the warewasher's output.

Of all the tasks in a professional kitchen, dishwashing must be the one least pondered or understood by the dining public. This is largely because few patrons realize that dirty dishes don't pile up until night's end as they do in old movies, in which deadbeat customers are forced to wash them as barter for their meal. Rather, they are cleaned and returned to the dining room *during* service. In other words, the plate from which one guest is polishing off their main course when you enter a restaurant may well be the same one on which yours will be served an hour later. Consequently, dishwashers are among the most essential and appreciated workers in a restaurant, and any chef or cook will tell you that if the dishwashing department goes down, it doesn't take long for a chain reaction to crash every other system. It's a fact of life that cooks and even sous chefs and chefs de cuisine come and go, but chefs will try their damnedest to keep a dependable dishwasher with them for as long as possible, even asking them to accompany them to their next place of employment. This isn't lost on Blanca and Hector. When I tell them, as prologue to our separate interviews, that I want to include them in this book because I believe their work is indispensable and underrecognized, both nod emphatically, as if to say, "Hey, tell us something we *don't* know."

Dishwashing is also the most common portal. For every Blanca and Hector likely to continue in this position, or a similar one, for the rest of their working days, there's a teenager who found themself washing dishes because it was one of the few jobs available to somebody their age, felt at home in the professional kitchen, and followed it into the cooking life, as much for love of the environment as interest in food. That a greater percentage of the Wherewithall team didn't wash dishes at some point is an exception to the norm; still, Reuben spent time in that position early in his career, and Johnny began as a dishwasher, as did David Lund, the former Parachute sous chef currently fulfilling Goldbelly orders. "I was just a high school kid looking for an afterschool job," David says of a part-time gig at Glen Loch Mill restaurant near his childhood home in Syracuse, New York. David sees irony in the dirty, wet work of dishwashing drawing fresh blood into the industry. "You'd think it would be a deterrent, that most people wouldn't want it," he says. A decent if indifferent student with natural aptitude for cooking, David had considered educational and career paths in forensic science and the military, but restaurants proved irresistible: the cacophony, the opportunity to work with his hands, and to *not* be imprisoned in an office cubicle gazing into the void of a computer screen. Of all the kitchen people interviewed for this book, David was also the only one who mentioned a virtue often lauded by the late Anthony Bourdain: "The kitchen is the last meritocracy—a world of absolutes," Bourdain once wrote. "One knows without any ambiguity at the end of each day how one did." David appreciated that as a dishwasher you had to "earn your dirt," and saw parallels in professional cooking: "You can see yourself getting better if you're trying and working on it," he says. "It's also one of those things where the proof is in the pudding: If something is good and tasty, and looks good—it *is*."

For Blanca, though, dishwashing *followed* cooking. As for Hector, he isn't technically a dishwasher. He's the restaurant's polisher, which means just what it sounds like: He polishes glasses by hand, so they are as clear and cloudless as any guest would expect. In practice, the job is more expansive than that. He has, as he puts it to me (proudly and in Spanish), "a big responsibility." He's constantly hauling plates, glasses, and kitchen equipment up and down stairs and replenishing those items around the kitchen and dining room. When possible, just as Jenna will contribute on the hot line, he also helps Blanca and Manuel clean.

Like Blanca, Hector left family—in his case, a wife and two grown children—in Ecuador and sends them the bulk of his earnings. Back home, Hector worked construction, building houses, but grew bored. He took advantage of his Chicago reboot to switch to restaurant work, though will still pick up an occasional hard-hat shift when he gets the call. He loathes complacency, and wants to please Beverly and Johnny, whom he appreciates for their acknowledgment of the entire staff. For him, the busier the restaurant, the more chances to validate his presence there and in the United States. When things really pick up, he maintains calm by ruminating on what this job—and country—have made possible for him: a house and car back in Ecuador, a car here in Chicago in which he gets to and from work in a quick fifteen minutes, and the ability to have provided his children a proper education and the chance for an easier and more professionally fulfilling life than his. So Hector must be inwardly elated right now, because the restaurant is approaching full tilt: As he climbs the stairs for the who-knows-which time tonight, the din hits him

Reuben and Thomas ready for an ambitious plate-up.

harder than when he headed down just a few minutes prior. He swerves past Jenna, rounding the corner into the kitchen, the dining room visible over the pass. The effect is that of passing through a stadium gate into the glare of lights over a night game. He maneuvers around Reuben and sets the dinner plates on the steel shelf over the stove, then reverses course and hurries back downstairs.

In the dining room, Black Joe Lewis & the Honeybears' "Sugarfoot"—a funky, James Brown-ish joint—kicks in on the sound system.

The kitchen has reached its weekly crescendo. It had to. The restaurant hasn't been this full in more than a year, with parties at all stages of a meal sharing the same space, their voices coalescing into a song, the silver- and glassware supplying percussion. It is the restored sound of restaurant normalcy. They will savor it later. For now, success means keeping pace. Everyone devotes mind and body to individual tasks, executing with precise, snappy movements. Jenna deposits two plates of crudité on the pass; Tayler immediately dispatches Griffin to deliver them to a freshly seated table. On the hot line, the appetizer course for a six-top reaches the end of its stationary assembly line as Reuben spoons sliced baby corn rounds over each of a half-dozen bowls; Thomas chases after him, arranging a wreath of bronze fennel fronds around the yolk on each portion, and up on the pass go the bowls. Tayler nods at Carly and José. They each pick up three bowls. "Table 16," says Tayler, and off Carly and Griffin race.

After weeks of knocking off the rust, the kitchen has located its rhythm and is in full collective flight. There will be no more lulls tonight. No chances to chug from a water bottle, or hit the bathroom. The next break will come after the last dessert has been served.

Reuben's on his knees, returning the Lexan of egg yolks to the lowboy refrigerator. Thomas has already started tempering portions of hake for the next batch to be cooked and plated.

Tayler scans the expediting sheets. Table 12 will be ready for their meat course any minute, as will three other tables. She calls to Thomas and Reuben: "Fire twelve meat."

Thomas nods, turns toward the oven.

"And a heads up," says Tayler, looking back down at the sheets. Thomas stops, turns. "We're going to fire eight more *right* after that."

Thomas nods again and gets to work.

Reuben stands, surveys the hot line: All is, for the moment, well in hand. The pass is utterly vacant. There's a lane to be exploited, and this once-and-future chef is the only one who's noticed.

"Should we do twenty at once?" he asks.

The others reel at his audacity.

"*Can* you do twenty?" asks Johnny, shouting to be heard over the Honeybears' horn section.

Reuben looks to Thomas, his superior in the chain of command, who solemnly nods his approval. The two of them look at Johnny and Tayler and, in unison, answer: "Yeah."

Twenty plates in the rearview mirror is gold on a Saturday night; Johnny and Tayler seize the opportunity: *"Do it!"*

Tayler monitors the uptick in action and pace: Reuben deals out twenty freshly arrived plates, still warm from the warewasher, on the counter in three uneven rows as Thomas removes a tray holding the strip loin from the oven and swiftly slices the pieces into four-ounce portions.

Jessica and the servers congregate at the pass, stealing time to watch this plate-up, the most ambitious production of its kind since the restaurant reopened. Beverly, having left their children back home with a sitter, has just returned, entering the dining room from the bar. Jessica whispers in her ear, letting her know what's going on. Beverly perks up, joining the staff spectators.

As Johnny taught them to earlier this week, the team have instinctively divvied up plating tasks: Reuben holds a tray of halved, partially dehydrated tomatoes with one hand, and arranges a tomato just off center on each plate with the other. Jenna, having heard the call of "fire *twenty* meat," has temporarily rejoined the hot line, and stands ready with a saucepan and ladle; as the tomatoes go down, she spoons red wine reduction over each one, letting it spill over into the center of the plate. Also working by hand, Thomas sets a strip-loin portion beside the tomato on each plate, atop the sauce pooled there. Finally, Johnny bats cleanup with the Lexan of sorrel leaves, topping and leaning them over and against the beef.

"Sugarfoot" gives way to "Champaign, Illinois," a honky-tonk anthem by Old 97's to the city just a little way downstate. Amid a symphony of hard-driving guitar chords and drumbeats, front man Rhett Miller croons about squandered lives, bourbon-soaked memories, and how if you play your cards right, "you will not go to Heaven, you'll go to Champaign, Illinois."

As Johnny silently okays each completed plate, Reuben and Thomas set them up on the pass, and Tayler dispatches servers, completing X's on the expediting sheet as she does:

"Carly, take four to Table 8."

"José, take three to Table 4."

Old 97's rocks out. The jam blankets the dining room.

"Nooshâ, those two to Table 12."

Nooshâ takes the plates in hand, turns, checks that her path is clear, and walks briskly to the table. As she arrives, the couple halt their conversation and look up expectantly.

"Dry-aged strip loin with tomato and sorrel," she says, setting the plates down, then turns and heads back to the pass, where other dishes wait.

Afterword

Wherewithall restaurant, as depicted in these pages, hasn't existed in quite some time. Most of the principal characters had pushed off long before this book was finished—either to other restaurants, new careers, and/or different cities. By spring 2023, of those profiled, only Beverly, Johnny, and Tayler remained. This is the nature of restaurants. Employees come and go in shifting pursuit of self, happiness, and prosperity, usually sooner than later.

It's also the nature of restaurants to close. With few exceptions, all of them, like Broadway shows, eventually will shutter. The brisk business and attendant optimism Wherewithall enjoyed on July 24, 2021, lasted for several months. Then came COVID's Omicron wave, which pulled the rug out from under the American restaurant industry during the holiday season. The cruel timing deprived owner-operators of much-needed revenue during what are traditionally, and by a good margin, the most profitable two months of any year, resulting in a fresh round of temporary and permanent closures. After that, for reasons Johnny and Beverly were unable to decode, Wherewithall never recovered its mojo. Then, in May 2023, came the death blow: The sewer line from the restaurant collapsed under the city street, rendering Wherewithall inoperable. Unable to afford a repair estimated in the tens of thousands, Beverly and Johnny finally pulled the plug.

It could have been worse: They own the building, and so are concepting and raising the relatively modest sum of money required to revivify the space with a new concept.

There *was* magic in the night we witnessed, when it seemed a sure bet that Wherewithall would power over the hump and endure, maybe even thrive, for years to come. Sometimes we have the luxury of saying goodbye around a hospital bed; other times there comes a shocking phone call informing us that a loved one is suddenly gone. Wherewithall went suddenly.

The restaurant now exists only in diaspora. Its cooks and chefs continue to apply and pass along skills and ideas learned and honed there. Still, after enough time goes by, it's more likely than not that Wherewithall, like most restaurants, will be lost to the ages. But what happened there will be subsumed into the industry's communal mind, and echo in dishes yet to be conceived.

Acknowledgments

Great thanks to the following friends, family, colleagues, and former strangers who let me into their worlds, or helped me out when I needed it.

My editor, Peter Hubbard, for first believing in the book in the dark days of 2020, and then offering crucial support, wisdom, and patience along the way. I will never forget it.

My friend and agent, David Black, who never gives up, and who lovingly badgered me into having a "getting to know you" call with Peter when it was the last thing I wanted to do. Without that call, this book wouldn't exist, at least not now.

The team at Wherewithall, especially Johnny Clark, Beverly Kim, and Tayler Ploshehanski. And to José Villalobos for being my translator for two interviews. Thank you all for your generous participation in this project. It was a privilege observing and getting to know you.

The farmers, purveyors, and workers profiled in this book, who graciously made time for me. And to their teams, especially Kayla Biegel, Steve Freeman, and Nick Nichols.

Thanks also to copyeditor Suzanne Fass (aka my human safety net) whose care, smarts, and fact-checking have saved me many embarrassing moments across several books. And to the team at HarperCollins: associate editor Molly Gendell, production manager Kimberly Kiefer, production editor Stephanie Vallejo, interior designer Renata DiBiase, cover designer Brian Moore, marketing director Kelly Dasta, and publicist Lindsey Kennedy.

For their help with permissions for the song lyrics quoted in the epigraph, great thanks to John Campanelli, Todd Ellis, Andalyn Lewis, F. Richard Pappas, and Carrie Tanner.

My longtime transcriber and the best, funniest sister-in-law on Earth, Sharon Saalfield.

The home team: Caitlin, Declan, and Taylor. I love and treasure you, and I'm glad this book takes place on your shared birthday, kids.

To my dog, Hudson, who passes what would otherwise be unbearably solitary days and nights at my feet.

They who know why: Greg Baxtrom, John Bravakis, David Cassidy, Diego Galicia and Rico Torres, Caroline Glover, James Gregorio, Max Katzenberg, Barbara Kopple, Steve Kroopnick, Gabe McMackin, Chandra

Ram and Jay Wilder, Hanna Raskin, Julia Sullivan, and Douglass Williams.

To friends who took the time to read all or part of the manuscript in various stages and share valuable feedback: Lauren Bloomberg, Scott Gramling, and David Waltuck.

I'd also be remiss not to acknowledge the influence and inspiration of John McPhee; the journalists and broadcasters who've covered me and my work over the years; readers of my books; listeners of my *Andrew Talks to Chefs* podcast, especially those who have taken the time to write and/or say hello at restaurants and conferences; and S.Pellegrino, especially Filippo Mazzaia and Michele Vieira, who have supported the podcast and me personally in ways large and small for several years.

And to anyone I might have forgotten: I'm sorry. Drinks on me next time.

About the Author

Andrew Friedman is the author of *Chefs, Drugs and Rock & Roll: How Food Lovers, Free Spirits, Misfits and Wanderers Created a New American Profession* (2018), and producer and host of the independent podcast *Andrew Talks to Chefs*. He is also the author of *Knives at Dawn: America's Quest for Culinary Glory at the Legendary Bocuse d'Or Competition* (2009), co-editor of the internationally popular anthology *Don't Try This at Home: Culinary Catastrophes from the World's Greatest Chefs* (2005), and co-author of more than twenty-five cookbooks, memoirs, and other projects with some of the United States' finest and most well-known chefs. Additionally, he is an adjunct professor within the School of Graduate and Professional Studies at the Culinary Institute of America. An avid tennis player, he co-authored American tennis star James Blake's *New York Times* bestselling memoir *Breaking Back: How I Lost Everything and Won Back My Life* (2007), and was for several years a *TENNIS* magazine editor-at-large. He lives in Brooklyn, NY.